Contents

Introduction

From Complacency to Conviction: My Sabbath Journey

Well, well—I thought I was well advanced in my walk with the Lord. How could I not be? I was raised Catholic, and after navigating my way out of that tradition, I felt confident I was on the right path. But life has a way of surprising us, doesn't it?

Denominations—a vast landscape of beliefs and practices—beckoned me. From **Congregational, Non-Denominational,** and **Protestant** to **Baptist** and even the spirited embrace of **Pentecostal** worship, I explored them all. As long as they held Jesus as our Savior, surely I couldn't go wrong.

Then came the revelation. Unbeknownst to me, I was about to embark on an unexpected adventure—one that would reveal my spiritual complacency. I had settled into what I now call a **Comfy Cozy religious system**—a place we're warned to avoid. I was sure I was saved but was my salvation truly working within me? The answer, I discovered, was far from comforting.

Barely awake one morning, I was struck by a heavy thought: "Shouldn't I be able to easily recite the Ten Commandments in order?" How could I claim to live for God when I didn't even know His commandments by heart, let alone in order? They should roll off my tongue as easily as the alphabet.

I walked down the hall toward the plaque of the Ten Commandments I had hung years ago. As my eyes adjusted and my mind began to clear, I stood before the simple plaque on my kitchen wall, its engraved words etched into my conscience:

1. Do not honor any other gods before Me.

2. You shall make no idols.

3. Do not take the Lord thy God's name in vain."

And then, there it was—**Commandment Number Four**. It was as if the heavens themselves whispered its significance into my soul. The discovery marked the beginning of a journey I had never anticipated—one that would prove to be powerful, transformative, and utterly life-changing.

The Sabbath—that sacred day of rest—captured my heart. Week after week, I observed it faithfully. And in that rhythm, I found blessings beyond measure. In the seventh week—my seventh kept Sabbath—marked a turning point. I couldn't keep this revelation to myself. I had to share the Good News, penning this small memoir.

Prepare to witness the profound impact of honoring this sacred day. The gateway to truth stands wide open, and though it may leave your head spinning at times, it promises to be the most exhilarating experience for every child called by our Creator. From doctrinal debates to the very names of our God and Messiah, recognizing the Old Testament as the foundation of the entire book is essential and cannot be neglected.

So, dear reader, travel with me through these pages. Witness my growth, my struggles, and the profound impact of honoring the Holy Day we are called to remember. For seasoned believers, this journey will resonate. And for those new to Sabbath keeping, may this memoir illuminate your path as you walk with your Father.

First Sabbath Day

Let us begin with a prayer:

Oh Heavenly Father, guide my words as I write this memoir. May my writing be divinely inspired, conveying Your truth and glorifying You.

In Jesus' name. Amen.

Newly Discovered: A Journey of Spiritual Awakening

The best way to start is to take a look at the commandment itself. Some facts about the **Sabbath** commandment are:

- We are told to remember it

- It specifies a particular day

- It has been around since creation

- It is a gift to us

- It is blessed

- It is a symbol of the contract between us and God

- When Jesus came He honored it

- The apostles kept it before and after Jesus ascended

- It will be kept until the end of time

- It is mentioned around 172 times in the Old Testament and about 60 times in the New Testament

- My favorite fact: It made it to the top 10!!!

The 4th Commandment:

Exodus 20:8-11

"Remember the Sabbath day, to keep it holy. Six days shalt thou labor, and do all thy work: But the seventh day is the sabbath of the LORD thy God: in it thou shalt not do any work, thou, nor thy son, nor thy daughter, thy manservant, nor thy maidservant, nor thy cattle, nor thy stranger that is within thy gates: For in six days the LORD made heaven and earth, the sea, and all that in them is, and rested the seventh day: wherefore the LORD blessed the sabbath day, and hallowed it."

The core aspects the 4th commandment instructs us to observe are:

- **Remember the Sabbath day.**

- **Keep this day holy and set apart.**

- **Complete your work and regular labor in 6 days.**

- **Do no work or have others do work on the Sabbath day.**

- **Rest from work just as God did after Creation.**

- **Honor the Sabbath as a blessed and sanctified time.**

While others may feel liberty in shifting designated days of sacred rest, I discovered a holiness uniquely birthed at Creation's close—which as I understand (at this time) to be Friday's sunset to Saturday's sunset. I share my story, not to debate which day is right, but simply to convey my found truth—grounded in what Genesis poetically frames as hallowed time, set apart with boundaries both protective and bursting with divine promise.

Having casually dismissed the 4th commandment most of my Christian walk, an unexpected nudge compelled me towards a season of intentional Sabbath observance. What first motivated me proved not legalistic obedience but rather a thirst for intimacy with God as He intended.

While this memoir features glimpses of my struggles reconciling long-held assumptions about the Sabbath from hearsay preachings, the aim remains to compellingly portray its tangible blessings when lived wholeheartedly.

What unfolded through these 7 faithful Sabbaths astonished me with newfound understanding. I already know this will be a new way of life for me from here on out—literally to the end of time. As this spiritual friendship with the Lord blossoms beautifully, my hunger increases steadily to share the message of abiding in the Sabbath.

Let's be real—my previous 'Sabbath days', which were on Sundays, were such half-hearted attempts, the Lord himself probably shook his head in disappointment seeing my feeble efforts unfold! Caught up binge-watching Netflix for hours on end, running errands all over town, or snoozing the daylight away; honoring God didn't feel remotely like my so-called day of **prioritized rest!** Somehow through God's grace, I finally started questioning why I never reflected on how this concept of sacred rest existed long before the 10 commandments—in Eden. Can you believe I almost lived my whole faithful life completely missing how this gift connects to God's original plan for human design and happiness?

My unexpected walk into the joy of deeming time itself now as holy—with the hope that you, brothers and sisters soon join the dance towards soul restoration God passionately prescribed. Whatever your doctrinal learning, I urge you to not dismiss the Sabbath loosely but daring to walk weeks ahead in experiential discovery through God's original desire of rest deeper than dogma.

A Beginner's Tale: Friday Morning Preparations

Journal Entry: The familiar fragrance of coffee permeates my kitchen, stirring anticipation on this morning that feels different from mundane weekly routines. Waking up on my first designated Sabbath preparation day feels comforting and curious all at once. Through my window, I notice birds hopping merrily from tree to tree, feeder to feeder, and squirrels scampering about the woods seemingly more chipper than usual. Nature's energy mirrors my own quiet celebration this morning—a hint of anticipatory joy stirring inside, expecting something special beyond the usual day's end. Mother Nature's mood mirrors my childlike awe—that wide-eyed wonder each sunrise holds.

While I aim for continual fellowship with God throughout each week, today's dawn feels especially magical—perhaps because I'm intentionally establishing this day apart solely for focused time with Him without normal busy work obligations creeping in as a priority. This sense of cleared schedules permits me to retreat into spiritual connection, liberating my mind from habitual multitasking tendencies. In essence, I've given myself the grand declaration to shove aside anything less important and soak up His presence without distraction. Our Father basically gives us a hall pass to ignore chores for the day—hallelujah!

If we do not **intentionally** schedule time for getting away from all the busyness and distractions to get to know God more, we start losing sight of why we were created and how deeply we are loved—it's about the intention.

What better weekly reboot than returning to our First Love—the ultimate gift my soul needs to align its perspective and priorities with the eternal, rather than the temporary secular concerns of this world.

My first dilemma rears its head. Okay, it's more of a luxury problem, but nonetheless, it's a situation I need to figure out. I had preexisting beach plans with friends made before feeling spiritually nudged towards observing the Sabbath. As I said, this is not a bad issue to have by any means; it's just that I've thoroughly dismissed the fourth commandment over the years, observing a casual "rest day" on my terms. Now, I have to make room in my life to ensure the Sabbath goes off without a hitch. These plans have now brought this awareness to the forefront, and not knowing the rules of the Sabbath, I'm about to cancel all plans!

My mind swims... (get it, thinking of the beach? Okay, never mind). Should I press pause on these social commitments and redirect my focus towards whatever Sabbath preparations entail? My brief online search mentions food preparation and putting your household in order. I seriously have no idea what that means other than pre-cooking your meals, maybe? So, I decide to move ahead as scheduled, joining my friends shore-side for distraction and fellowship.

Why should I feel obligated to dedicate this entire Friday to intensive spiritual preparations instead of enjoying previously scheduled relaxation with friends? After all, many people complete full work days before transitioning to embrace the Sabbath at sunset. There is no way the entire Sabbath-keeping world takes every Friday off of work to prepare. If they can sufficiently shift gears amid busy vocations without full-day preparation, perhaps I too can reconcile maintaining everyday commitments today while still welcoming the holy hours at sunset.

What a beautiful beach day! I am here with my friends, enjoying the warm sun, gentle breezes, and the sounds of crashing waves and chirping seagulls. My mind wanders, though... Should I share with them why I'll soon have to leave? I know the minute I start to pack up early, they'll ask questions—they are a ~~nosey~~ caring bunch. I can hear it already: if I announce departing to prepare for Sabbath, mouths will drop in surprise.

I just don't have the bandwidth right now to respond while I'm actively trying to figure this out myself in these beginning days. God called me into rediscovered intimacy through keeping this holy observance anew, and I responded — that foundation remains my compass, not others' confusion over changing routines. For today, our fun continues soaking in this seaside carefree company and the blissful beach backdrop embracing us. The bright sun dazzles, wind a sweet relief from gathering heat — Inhaling deeply, I breathe in all the gratitude before nightfall ushers in a sacred refuge.

Flip flops on sandy feet — I pack up my beach blanket as the evening sun heads toward the horizon. There's plenty of time for a quick grocery run to grab some easy food prep options in anticipation of this first-ever Sabbath kickoff tonight! Watermelon slices, salad fixings, maybe a veggie plate? Items that require minimal preparation seem wise, given that

I'm a newcomer, assuming that cooking is prohibited on the Sabbath. All I know so far is this holy time should center on God, not growling stomachs or poor planning! Note to self: you cannot use this as an excuse to eat prepackaged foods such as cookies and chips. I'm embarking on this new adventure to grow spiritually, not physically-wide.

20 minutes until sundown! My house is quiet, the mood is set: blinds closed, little lamps on, TVs and electronics about to shut off. Wait!!! Can I shower on the Sabbath? Maybe I should take a quick shower before the sun is no longer. I will have to learn as I go on this journey. I'm aware this should be a non-stressful experience for us and I refuse to let legalistic rituals become a part of this new relationship. The character of God that I know wants us to enjoy this as a blessing, not a curse.

The sun is setting!!! I take a deep breath, saturated with peace. I wonder what awaits. As soon as the sun goes down, I am sure to feel a welcoming restoration. Bye, for now, my friends, as I need to focus on Him. Enjoy your Sabbath rest. Peace and blessings!

Let's close with a word of prayer:

Dear God,

Thank you for bringing this newfound gift to our attention. For working in our hearts and leading our desires to do Your will.

Please bless us with Your wisdom and truth so we can wonderfully serve You.

Let this week reflect the love You have shown us today and give us opportunities to share that Love and plant seeds.

In Jesus' name. Amen.

Second Sabbath Day

Let's start with prayer:

Heavenly Father,

Bless this holy Sabbath day with Your presence. Let us find fellowship, wisdom, and peace. As we approach tonight's rest in You, allow the world's distractions to dissipate so our hearts and minds surrender completely to what You wish to reveal.

Let us humbly come before You, knowing that through Your grace alone we found the gift of salvation. Give us eyes to see and ears to hear. Nourish our bodies with the food You provided and our souls with Your precious Word.

In Jesus' name. Amen.

Reflections - Information Overload

Last week's Sabbath was such a blessing to me, but it definitely did not end at sunset on Saturday. I found that I was busier than ever exploring new insights — Saturday's topics went well into the following week. It was a lot of information at once and somewhat overwhelming, but welcomed.

I believe as we draw nearer to the Lord, our thirst for knowledge becomes insatiable. Disregard the fact that I feel significantly behind, having only now come to see the truth.

This Bible, once familiar, now seems like an entirely new book once your eyes are opened. You comprehend its depths, and the truths unveiled are boundless. Pray for God to reveal His truth to you before you open your Bibles—He will honor that prayer.

Friday Night

Journal Entry: Friday's sunset was around 8 pm, I was already tired from the day so tonight's invitation to rest actually sounded better than going out. So far, this second attempt at a Friday Sabbath night seems pretty peaceful rather than some intense spiritual challenge. I'm not saying setting time aside for Sabbath should feel like a challenge, yet I can see how there will be a time sooner or later when I will be tested to do something. After all, think about it, the world has made Friday and Saturday the two most important days for entertainment, parties, celebrations, etc...

All I know is this intentional God-and-me timeout felt beyond needed. Now, I wish everyone grasped how to access this for themselves without complicated layers mucking things up. But even wanting to share moments can shift your focus if not mindful.

I do feel at a loss at this moment — I have no one in my life that honors a Sabbath, not one. I enter into this newness as uneducated as a baby and completely alone. I am fine with being alone, well alone in a secular sense, not a spiritual sense. Still though, having some soul tribe kinship alongside this journey of mine intrigues me. Someday I'll find my people — we'll see!

I probably should have done my homework prior to entering into tonight's commandment experience to understand what activities God is actually cool with during this Holy Day. But I have to be honest — it hits me now how even usual habits like watching shows or scrolling could distract me from the priceless opportunity at hand: An appointed time to meet with God.

Unfortunately, I will grab my phone as it is a way for me to enter this Sabbath world from my living room. I searched "live bible studies" and found so much fellowship on this particular platform. Real worship entered my house. I cried, prayed, and felt so close to the Lord, that I didn't want it to end.

The people in the group were saying things like "happy Sabbath" and "Shabbat Shalom" which I have no idea what that means, yet! Truly, I was without conviction using my phone because this new virtual room was packed with Sabbath-keeping veterans. The Bible studies I encountered were deeply thorough and captivating. It was my first experience where scripture was the powerful force and not man's interpretations. I actually reached for my Bible that had been neglected way too long, ouch!!!

I've found that many of us are alone in our geographical areas, without people to commune with. Many are just coming to the truth, just like us. Wow! When the Holy Spirit moves, He moves. I suppose we just have to be in a place where we are humble and our heart posture is aligned to hear Him speak to us.

As one study ended another one started and the night passed by rather quickly, I am enjoying it so much, but oh the folly...as Paul warned, blessings and curses spring from the same mouth, in this case, the same platform.

The peace filling me merely minutes before fled rapidly amid the hateful speech. Honestly, the enemy wastes no time stirring chaos! Too good to be true? No — too spiritually discerning to miss the telltale strategy. I mean what better way to distract brothers and sisters from learning what God has for them other than to get them arguing?

I think we all know our Father's refining process may not always be easy, but He will assuredly carry us through. I say this because we might be up against opposition, attacks, and deception, as well as knowledge and growth.

Scrolling through social rooms to find fellowship, and having witnessed brothers and sisters laboring tirelessly all night on single topics, debating as if engaged in a competition, was seriously upsetting. Be mindful that honoring the Sabbath day can attract opposition; perhaps that's why I'm keeping it to myself at the moment. Interacting with strangers is challenging enough...lol.

If you are one of those who believe that when you're about to engage in God's work or encounter His truth, the enemy will attack and try to cause confusion, you are absolutely correct. A Scripture that comes to mind is...

1 Corinthians 14:33

"For God is not the author of confusion but of peace, as in all the churches of the saints."

This verse affirms that God's heart seeks order, coherence, and clarity rather than disarray and turmoil. By implication, confusion originates from fallen/opposing sources.

1 Corinthians 14:40

"Let all things be done decently and in order."

In God's household, the Spirit models and mandates orderly, understandable proceedings rather than tolerating things being convoluted or bewildering. This, too, hints that forces countering His purposes stir mayhem.

I'm feeling overwhelmed as controversial doctrinal debates resurface regarding matters like salvation theology, adherence to God's commands, the trinity, Sabbath-keeping practices, law vs grace salvation frameworks, and conflicting rapture sequence views (pre-trib, mid-trib, post-trib).

As statements grew increasingly pointed, that saying came to mind — "ignorance is bliss" and is wearing new dimensions now. What am I setting myself up for by braving deep waters? These disputes carry such gravity for some seekers, entire identities anchored arguing angles, brothers, and sisters get utterly caught up trying to prove, and that to me is more about pride rather than sincere truth-seeking. Yes, diligent scriptural examination proves paramount, but this chaos reflected more heart matters.

Please remember that we are called to love one another above everything else. Let's not turn against each other creating distractions from where they need to stay — with HIM. It's really okay to meet people where they are on their walk and love them to the truth.

Feeling overwhelmed processing so many competing doctrines today, I just needed to power down fully and rest in calming worship music for a while to recharge spiritually and mentally. Shutting off all screens and bright lights to relax with delightful music, I curled up gratefully letting peace wash away the tension piled on by all those debates.

Saturday's Calm

Journal Entry: Waking up Saturday morning, a deep sense of calm and quietness fills me up. I feel so peaceful, humble, and untroubled within. My spirit feels tranquil, my mind serene — a humbling quietness within me.

Well, that didn't last long. I'm staring at my unmade bed (assuming it's a chore that cannot be done) and I am contemplating making it. I know, I know, another luxury problem. I can hear the Father's voice gently letting me know my overly-tidiness tendencies will have to be put aside for Him. I have a hard time resting or getting into a project while one is unfinished. This should be easy, right? I leave it unmade and I stroll down the hallway on a mission to start my coffee pot and open the blinds (I believe it's okay to do these things) while all along I have Ezekiel, my half chihuahua, half Pomeranian at my heels. Yes, his dad's name was Samson and his mom's name was Delilah. What better place than the Bible to come up with some unique dog names? Dogs are so reliant on us to provide their every need, they are literally at our mercy and spend their entire lives aiming to please us. It is how we should be with our Lord and Savior — we could learn from that type of dependency and loyalty, for sure.

Coffee is brewed and Ezekiel and I take ourselves out onto the porch where we can enjoy the morning sun and serenity. "Hey Google, play worship music!" As I'm swaying back and forth in the rocking chair, sipping coffee, and listening to worship music, I am reflecting on last night and looking forward, to the day ahead.

In Search of Truth: Examining Beliefs through Scripture

Just in 2 short weeks, after I started Sabbath keeping, I heard things I'd never heard before or learned that what I thought was right was not. I'm sharing these matters because I believe, and have confirmed with others, that when we encounter truth, we all go through a similar transformation process. It's a lot of knowledge to absorb at once, and it can be overwhelming. Not only am I realizing that the church has significantly diluted the scriptures, but they've also outright lied to us. We must pray for wisdom because along with learning the truth, we will also face attempts by the enemy to distort that new knowledge. Now more than ever, we NEED to study to "**show ourselves approved.**" Nine out of ten of us never really did this, and without verifying what we hear in scripture, we **will** be deceived again - that same ole serpent twists the truth every time. He **seeks to destroy** us, just like a **roaring lion.**

1 Peter 5:8

"Be alert and of sober mind. Your enemy the devil prowls around like a roaring lion looking for someone to devour."

This verse portrays the devil as actively seeking to destroy and compares his actions to a roaring lion prowling for prey. It serves as a warning to be vigilant and spiritually prepared against the adversary's schemes. The main reason why we need to verify everything with the Word.

2 Timothy 2:15

"Study to shew thyself approved unto God, a workman that needeth not to be ashamed, rightly dividing the word of truth."

This verse encourages believers to **diligently** study and correctly handle the Word of God, so they can be approved by God and effectively serve in His Kingdom. It underlines the importance of understanding and applying Scripture with accuracy and integrity.

Diligently and **rightly** handles the message of truth in the context of 2 Timothy 2:15.

1. **Diligently**: This suggests putting forth effort and earnestly applying oneself to the study and understanding of God's Word. It involves dedication, perseverance, and thoroughness in seeking to comprehend the teachings and principles found in Scripture.

2. **Rightly handles the message of truth**: This refers to accurately interpreting and applying the truths of Scripture. It involves skillfully and correctly dividing or interpreting the Word of God, ensuring that one's understanding and teaching align with the intended meaning and context of the biblical text. It emphasizes the importance of handling Scripture with care, avoiding misinterpretation or distortion, and faithfully conveying its intended message to others.

In essence, 2 Timothy 2:15 encourages believers to study and correctly apply the teachings of Scripture, ensuring that their understanding and application of God's Word are accurate and faithful.

Sunset's creeping up, and I am not thrilled about getting dragged back into regular life chaos once this peaceful Sabbath bubble pops. Can we freeze time for a few hours? I'm already looking ahead excitedly, imagining how next Friday might feel now that I am growing accustomed to everything these restful days offer.

Enjoy the rest of your sabbath day. Until next week... Be blessed and praise our Lord for He is worthy of all praises!

Closing prayer:

Lord God, we give You unending thanks, for You have brought us another Sabbath day gift. You have kept and blessed us from sunset to sunset. Please continue to bless us throughout this week and guide our steps each and every day. We look forward to meeting with you every day but especially the next Sabbath day.

In Jesus' precious name. Amen

Third Sabbath Day

Let us start with words of prayer:

As we enter this sacred day You've given us to set apart, let us remember that You, our Creator, are the reason we are here—to glorify and celebrate all that You have done and will do for us.

Forgive us of our trespasses and those who trespassed against us. May we learn from Your grace how to love others the way You love us.

Allow what we learn today to become opportunities to share Your love, Your gift, and Your never-ending desire to have us with You.

In Jesus' name. Amen

Friday's Sunset

Journal Entry: As the sun's descent ushered in this Friday evening I look forward to receiving the blessings the next 24 hours will bring.

I take intentional moments preparing nourishing plates and calming spaces, simultaneously wondering what are proper "Sabbath meals." I make a mental note to dig into traditional foods/meals for next week's return since my amateur instincts are sorely lacking. I am grateful for the later sunsets on these cooler summer Friday nights— I am still able to prepare my dinner meal without interrupting the Sabbath.

I had planned to meet up with an online live group of Sabbath-keeping people. Shabbat Shalom, (peaceful rest) they say — I'm so pleased to be aware of the tiniest bit of Sabbath lingo. My first thoughts about social media platforms last week left me feeling unsure and possibly convicted? This week I know how this avenue can and is being used for God and to grow His kingdom. I am blessed to have this option to fellowship.

Goals: gathering for a meal with like-minded people, and laughing and learning more about God. Sounds wonderful.

Oh, I have to mention last week's sabbath did NOT go unnoticed, as sentiments of peace trickled into and throughout the week — many concerned questions from multiple friends and family about my vanished availability throughout Saturday stirred complicated feelings. I longed to unveil this unexpected spiritual journey, but first I needed to create solid foundations before coaxing companions. At first, I felt impatient to share this glory behind the spiritual escape because I wanted company! I believe it is wise at this time to inspect my own soul without others mocking half-baked revelations. I must let certainty build resilience before revealing too much too soon. I'm too fragile for skepticism to crush my eagerness to learn.

A positive viewpoint, though, I found it powerful how the Sabbath affected my week ahead and rested in my soul for days to come. Come the subsequent seventh morning, I absolutely longed for spiritual renewal upon realizing the previous Sabbath serenity had somewhat faded. How quickly we drift when the flesh and world converge efforts trading peace for chaos.

For my new friends who are giving the Sabbath an initial try after last week's entry: Did you find some sweet tranquility, and did patience persevere longer after the Sabbath as well? I ask because as a new sabbath trainee, I don't expect to constantly maintain rest between Sabbath occasions. Maybe seasoned friends might! For me, I notice patience and purity dissipate amid life bombardments by midweek.

As I type this very line, 3 amazing weeks of eye-opening changes now enrich my story, and the realization of the importance of honoring this specific day — the Sabbath day....Praise God for fresh mercies awaiting us!

Until about midnight I was studying and actually ended up falling asleep while reading — slept like a baby.

Sabbath Mornings

Journal Entry: Good morning, Saturday! Happy Sabbath brothers and sisters. As I am writing this memoir, I think a lot about who will be reading it. Who are those who will be trying out the Sabbath for the first time? Will you use this book as a guide, for company and possibly comfort knowing you are not alone? Envision with me the rippling fellowship our stories will kindle as soul nourishes soul across cities and nations in solidarity through God's timeless gift, retrieved long at last!

Together as fellow learners, we lay down the tendency to define ourselves narrowly by our jobs/careers alone. Instead, our core identity gets remade more balanced as children of God each time we pause for holy rest and wonder what that Sabbath brings. Humans are created for connection and gathering with like-minded believers that fuel spiritual growth.

Hebrews 10:25

"Not neglecting to meet together, as is the habit of some, but encouraging one another, and all the more as you see the day drawing near."

Though online spaces provide some sense of Sabbath fellowship, nothing can fully replace face-to-face community, worship, and discussion for Sabbath-keepers seeking to grow. However, sometimes faith requires walking alone on God's path, but I know in my heart that finding others to walk alongside would nourish and strengthen my Sabbath journey tremendously.

Returning to Saturday's events, I did spend time alone with the Lord, finishing my reading of the book of Acts, listening to worship music, and praying.

Always Was, Always Will Be

As I'm reading Acts, the early church history records believers gathering, preaching, and revering the seventh-day rest continually, with no controversy in sight. So why do Christians declare it was just for Israel and/or we rest in Jesus ("He is our rest") so there's no need to honor it now?

Scripture seems pretty straightforward. **Sabbath was established at Creation itself and then practiced faithfully throughout the epistles by Christ's example.** The bigger question becomes why we risk exhausting debates reasoning away commandments instead of following them for our spiritual well-being. There is evidence pointing to the **Sabbath celebration continuing in heaven's holy habitation once earth passes away.**

There are several passages that say the Sabbath always was and will always be:

Isaiah 66:22-23

"'For as the new heavens and the new earth, which I will make, shall remain before me,' saith the Lord, 'so shall your seed and your name remain. And it shall come to pass, that from one new moon to another,

and from one sabbath to another, shall all flesh come to worship before me,' saith the Lord.'"

This passage speaks of the new heavens and earth to come and describes all people coming to worship God from Sabbath to Sabbath even in the **new heavens and the new earth**.

Our future home awaits—a world where God's presence permeates every corner, and His light dispels all darkness. It is clear that from the beginning of creation to the new world when we walk with God, we will be honoring the Sabbath! What an honor!

In essence, set-apart Sabbath time facilitating intimacy with Creator God carries symbolic continuity **from this world into forever**, but it will no longer serve the teaching/learning function as direct unbroken fellowship becomes our eternal reality removing all veils!

Exodus 31:16-17

"The Israelites are to observe the Sabbath, celebrating it for the generations to come as a lasting covenant. It will be a sign between me and the Israelites forever, for in six days the Lord made the heavens and the earth, and on the seventh day he rested and was refreshed."

This passage from Exodus emphasizes that the Sabbath was established as a perpetual covenant between God and the people of Israel, signifying their relationship and God's creative power. It underscores the enduring nature of the Sabbath observance across generations as a sign of God's authority and rest.

The reason stated for Sabbath's origins here is timeless (supporting human welfare across all generations), not temporary or fulfilled by Christ. As we saw in Isaiah, there are verses that back up that Sabbath keeping will continue on the new earth. Also, many verses show that even Jesus and His apostles honored the Sabbath as well, even after Jesus ascended, and He knew they would continue keeping the Sabbath.

Matthew 24:20

"But pray ye that your flight be not in the winter, neither on the sabbath day."

As we see in **Matthew 24:20** it talks about, let it not happen in winter or on the Sabbath day. Jesus was warning them about the destruction of the temple in 70 AD meaning **He was expecting us all to keep the Sabbath day well after his ascension.**

Jesus advises his followers to pray that their flight (escape) does not happen on the Sabbath day. This is because traveling long distances or engaging in activities during the Sabbath could potentially make their escape more challenging. Jesus emphasizes the importance of being spiritually prepared and mindful of religious observances even in times of crisis.

There exist zero contextual clues suggesting Sabbath provisions somehow expired or ceased importance once Jesus came. It was rather the opposite!

Another point for us to ponder is this: during creation week, the Sabbath was instituted when Adam and Eve walked in the garden with our Creator. If the Sabbath was established as the last day of creation, then from that time until the fall (apple eating), we honored the Sabbath day with our Creator. It makes perfect sense to believe that we will do the same thing when we are living in the new world with Him. I think the garden life is the way He wanted it from the beginning, so I imagine we will have that garden restored for eternity, and He will walk among us. I can't wait!

Another point in regards to the Sabbath being instituted at the time of creation is, that this was before Israel, the people, were established. This means that it is intended for ALL of creation, not just the Israelites. Did God want His chosen to adopt this day of reverence? Yes! Did Jesus's death, burial, and resurrection give us the chance to become His chosen Israel? Yes!

In closing:

Blessings my friends, for a wonderful week. I am looking forward to being together in the Lord 7 nights from now.

Thank you, Lord! Again, we get to meet you on the day You appointed us. What a glorious time it is when we choose Your will over our own. Our willing hearts gladly embrace what the gift of this day has to offer.

Let us go into this week praising and serving You to the fullest. Protect us and our families as we enter into this week.

In Jesus' name. Amen

Fourth Sabbath Day

Opening Prayer:

Lord, as we approach the closing of this day and prepare to meet with You and our fellow Sabbath keepers, remind us of who You are - our Creator, Provider, Protector, Father, and Comforter. You are worthy of all our praises, and as we enter into the gift of a holy rest day, we ask for forgiveness of our sins as we humbly seek Your presence.

Thank You, Lord, for this day to rest our bodies, minds, and souls as we leave the world behind and step into Your light.

In Jesus' name. Amen.

Reflections

Welcome back, fellow sabbath keepers! What a week – again questions from many friends about my disappearance, lol...I never realized so many people kept such close track of my text delays and unanswered calls. It goes to show people do notice changes. How about you? Has anyone noticed that you're missing on Friday nights and Saturdays now, too?

Are you trying to figure out if this day remains binding for us to fully honor in obedience or not? For me personally, no matter the debates on either side, I cannot deny the **tremendous blessings** saturating each Sabbath celebration thus far. I simply have no desire to forfeit such spiritual nourishment and revelation found through this gift!

What are your initial thoughts on what Sabbath-keeping is at its core? A legalistic obligation we grit our teeth to fulfill out of fear or dread? Or a divine blessing and time with God we cheerfully prioritize as much as any other loved relationship because we cherish it? Right? Yes!

For me, just these short weeks welcoming the Sabbath have unveiled whole areas of life with new eyes — spiritually expanding exponentially compared to previously complacent decades, if I'm fully honest. I sense heavenly peace passing understanding (Philippians 4:7) ... suddenly feeling content rather than anxiously striving, less wrapped up in temporary matters and more wrapped in eternal perspective!

Have you noticed new fruits and a renewing since embracing the Sabbath and turning from worldly noise? Perhaps it begins subtly at first—or perhaps a total transformation happens overnight. For me, now that I pay more attention to the commands as a moral compass, I can clearly see where I need to change. I could be a little less gossipy, a little less judgy, and a lot less worldly. The Sabbath day has changed me, and I have a feeling it will continually bring about changes.

As the weeks passed, I faced some criticism regarding my Sabbath honoring — good ole 'persecution' as Scripture names it. At a minimum, I wish they'd approach differing views ready to learn rather than attacking what they haven't personally examined yet. What Christian heart clings so tightly to current assumptions that curiosity about broader truth gets suffocated?

Doesn't every spiritual infant at some point realize previous perspectives demand prayerful re-investigating? Through God's grace, we shift from happily regurgitating spoon-fed doctrine to maturity, carefully weighing new insights and recognizing blindspots exposed under a closer look.

This is why I'll always hear out alternate biblical explanations respectfully, not necessarily embracing every word but acknowledging the hunger for wisdom and humility before God's Word. We rest our security in teachable spirits unafraid of reform, not stubborn pride fortifying easy assumptions.

If anything, one eye-opening revelation I've gleaned from the past three Sabbath weeks is how little my personal scriptural research seems to have shaped my faith understanding up until now. I'm faced with realizing the bulk of my belief system seems to simply echo what others like pastors, more advanced church members, or even parents taught me as gospel without digging deeper to verify veracity.

Clearly, so much goes unchecked sliding neatly into inherited assumptions rather than being truly wrestled with. How much do I subconsciously outsource my own soul-searching for the truth to external voices without interrogating their perspectives myself? Do you suppose we all perhaps lean on convenient authorities more than we admit instead of earnest individual bible study? Who do you quickly begin trusting when confusion arises, your own prayerful studies or a favorite opinionated podcast instead? A podcast seems easier at that moment, but not worth the domino effect mistruths can have leading to false doctrine. Now that we have come this far, we can't be that irresponsible with God's Word.

Are you ultimately with me in this conviction that we must renew firsthand devotion to seeking the Word alone as our guiding light and lamp for each path ahead, relying on third-party guidance far less from here on out?

Friday's Sunset

Journal Entry: This Sabbath is about to get extra interesting, as hurricane warnings try to intrude on this holy day. As strong winds thrashed tree limbs angrily outside in nature's temper tantrum, I sang praises to He who hushes winds with a glance.

Candles lit and a water-filled tub preparing for possible powerless darkness ahead, though somehow that mattered little. Bible reading by candlelight sounded appealing.

I cherish this time, meditating on the Scriptures, and hearing His voice. Do you feel Him nearer, too? I am overjoyed you're here with me, enjoying the gift of this day—after all He created it for us :) And this is where I want to bring our focus tonight.

Debaters often claim, that the Sabbath was made for you, so you can do whatever you want — take it, leave it, make it whatever day you feel you need to rest. This oppositional statement is frequently directed at Sabbath keepers. Many mainstream churchgoers observe Sunday as their "God" day, which critics argue is self-serving and disobedient to Sabbath principles. Let's delve into the verse that underlies these discussions.

Mark 2:27

"And He said unto them, the Sabbath was made for man, and not man for the Sabbath."

"The sabbath was made for man..." Meaning, it exists as a gift of guidance and blessing for the well-being of humanity. Sabbath is given in service of nourishing people's needs, not arbitrary legalism. It affirms God established the Sabbath for mankind's benefit — as an institution crafted specifically for human well-being out of divine care and intention.

Moreover, the climax really comes in the second half of the verse, reorienting flawed thinking, "**and not man for the Sabbath.**"

Here Jesus aims at religious leaders treating Sabbath rules almost like a deity itself, rather than a gift liberating hearts towards connection with God alone. The fact that they think people exist for Sabbath rules, over rest and doing good, means they lost sight of its purpose entirely — intimate friendship.

The Sabbath should serve people's needs and well-being, not the other way around. It highlights the principle that religious laws and practices should enhance human life and dignity, rather than becoming oppressive or legalistic burdens.

Sabbath was **tailor-made** for human health, happiness, and holiness from the very first week of Creation onward (Genesis account). Yet somewhere along the way, additional restrictions piled on turning Sabbath observance into a legalistic source of exhaustion rather than the life-breathing gift always meant simply to reconnect mankind back to intimate friendship with their Creator regularly.

Jesus reminds critical religious leaders - that the heart behind this gift matters most. Rules serve people; people were not designed as slaves fruitlessly chasing restrictive rule-keeping alone - again relationship must come first!

These statements affirm that God instituting holy rest AT Creation specifically because we prosper most when aligning schedules to honor wisdom greater than exploitation tendencies.

Then when Jesus says He is **Lord over the Sabbath** He means He created it, again showing He was there at the beginning of creation. The fuller context grounds Jesus's conclusion — as Lord, His actions demonstrated the heart behind the Sabbath rather than seeking loopholes in commands simply because He technically held authority over it.

I believe that's why Jesus healed, and picked wheat to eat, because on the Sabbath day, to show the rule makers that we are still to love and care for people on this day. If we think of modern-day healthcare, law enforcement, firemen, and EMTs — people need care and help every day and we are allowed to do that. One pastor told me that his wife, a nurse who had to work on the Sabbath, would take that day's wages and give them to the needy. I thought that was amazing, she was working on the Sabbath but not getting paid, yet paying it forward. What a beautiful testimony to her love for the Father. All glory to Him!!!

This has been a night filled with blessings. The familiar crashing noises of the Carolina Coast have become a soothing percussion, like a comforting white noise lulling me towards sleep. Tears of gratitude overwhelm me as I find myself immersed in His love. I bid you all goodnight, sisters, and brothers! See you in the morning. Sleep well.

Saturday

Good Morning,

Journal Entry: It is Saturday and the world is calm out there, like a hurricane didn't even happen after all — it literally didn't, turned out to be a small storm in comparison to the usual "possible hurricane" warnings.

Of course, the day, as I am sure you could guess, starts with a piping hot cup of hazelnut coffee and doggy cuddles. Wrapped in a blanket, I take that first sip of comfort in a cup — the way the hot cup warms my hands when I hold it, I LOVE IT! There's nothing like that first sip feeling — the second cup never does taste the same.

It's getting easier and easier for me to put off the household chores and disregard notification circles all over my phone. Music softly plays in the background while I read and write dedications to this day.

As I pass by the window, I notice all the raking I did last week was pointless as there wasn't any cleared ground in sight; it's a blanket of leaves out there. I am tempted to go out with my leaf blower and tackle this instantly but it can wait... these things have to wait as I am reminding myself quickly that I am supposed to be resting today. Along with the layering of fallen dead leaves, I am aware the summer green has completely vanished, and my sunsets will arrive sooner, as clocks will fall back an hour and Friday's preparation window will be shortened.

As I close this sabbath day out, I take a deep breath knowing that I have to go into the world this week and again address once more why I am doing what I am doing. You'd think I was up to no good the way some are acting towards me. I have one friend writing to a pastor asking him about honoring the Sabbath. At first, I thought it was good that my friend was at least curious about it. However, I saw my past self in those actions. Curiosity = run to a pastor or friend. Nevertheless, I was anticipating the response and open to hearing what this pastor had to say. Well, that pastor's reply single-handedly kept my friend from an open mind and heart to even consider what I was saying. It then started a contagious condemnation towards me instead of the curiosity I thought it would bring. Apparently, my taking a day off from the world for the Lord's sake has welled up emotions or convictions in their hearts—only God knows.

It feels like an endless battle justifying Sabbath's relevance for today; friends react from places I can't control. I attempt to explain to them again unless one purposefully honors this gift through ceasing regular life elements and distractions, true rest stays sadly elusive even when claiming Jesus as the cornerstone.

As I said previously, if you pick your day of rest, is it really even a Sabbath rest, or just a day you're not working so you can catch up on your responsibilities?" And, by the way, who are we to pick OUR Sabbath day over when God tells us? It has to be the 7th day! We are full of ourselves, aren't we?

Another one of the classic comebacks is, that Jesus is our rest, so we rest in Him every day. Remember the commandment and what it literally says, "**Six days you shall labor and do all your work,**" therefore you cannot rest every day. Let's continue looking into this to see what "rest in Him" on the Sabbath means in fuller detail, of course.

Old Testament

Hebrew Insights: Sabbath = Shabbat

The word "Sabbath," used 169 times, literally translates as "ceasing, stopping, resting." The phrase "Shabbat Shabbaton" amplifies this to mean a solemn, ceremonial rest from mundane labors. God's "rest" after finishing creation in Genesis established this sacred pattern and vocabulary. What a powerful precedent!

New Testament

Hebrews 4:8-11

"For if Jesus had given them rest, then would he not afterward have spoken of another day. There remaineth therefore a rest to the people of God. For he that is entered into his rest, he also hath ceased from his own works, as God did from his. Let us labor therefore to enter into that rest, lest any man fall after the same example of unbelief."

Greek Insights: Sabbath Rest = Sabbatismos

Hebrews 4:8-11 connects spiritual rest with the idea of the Sabbath, but it doesn't cancel the importance of keeping the Fourth Commandment. Instead, it introduces a new Greek term, "Sabbatismos," which links the spiritual rest we find in Christ with the weekly Sabbath observance. This highlights that as believers we honor it out of obedience.

In fact, early believers endured immense persecution for obeying 10 commandments foundationally, including the seventh day Sabbath! Do you think they would endure such persecution if they didn't have to keep The Commandments/Sabbath Day? They absolutely knew it was expected of them to follow all 10 commandments to the best of their abilities. Not 1 or 2 commandments, not 9 commandments... TEN! **No biblical grounds justify dismantling the 4th commandment alone while upholding the other 9 for church-age application.**

As we discussed in the previous chapter, this is not merely a poetic metaphor but a prophetic promise. Isaiah (ch. 56) points to a future where all people grafted into spiritual Israel will continue observing the Sabbath, even physically, in the new heaven and new earth for eternity — rather than it being a temporary practice that has been discontinued. Praise God!

Resting In Him-On Purpose

Back to the people and that comment, "We rest in Jesus now so every day is a rest day" or "I can pick whatever day I want for my rest day." I challenge them to prepare and set out to honor Him on this day, the 7th day. The 7th day because He says, "remember" that day specifically. **You don't get to pick your own day.** Do not do anything else that day other than rest and honor the Creator. I guarantee they will find beauty here.

Without intending legalism, keeping Sabbath challenges evaluating whether our usual 'day off' patterns resemble mindful worship or just unchanged routines under a spiritualized label. When we merely sprinkle church in between habitual pastimes calling it honoring God's design for flourishing, have we awakened fully to holiness yet? I think not!

Will you seek out God's rest on purpose? Hopefully, your day of rest is more than you do you...church for a couple of hours, gym, play, movies, out to eat... That's your definition of rest, not our Father's. **Deliberately and intentionally setting out to do a particular thing on a particular day means everything and makes all the difference. Your will versus His will.** It is choosing the Lord, dedicating your day to Him in obedience and gratitude...your whole self partaking in the day for our Lord.

It has been another great and eventful Sabbath day with you, my friends. I don't expect we will all believe and see the same truths at the same time. I do believe we are all here because we wholeheartedly seek His truths. In Him, we will find them. Together we are learning about this new terrain.

Let's close with a loving word to our Father:

Our loving Father,

Thank You for bringing us together for fellowship, rest, and worship. Our love for You is overflowing and You are worthy to be praised for eternity.

Lord, dress us in Your mighty armor as we go out into the busy world this week. Send us opportunities to spread Your gift of salvation so that others may enjoy the blessings we have. Provide us with wisdom and discernment so we can walk fully in the Spirit- to have the knowledge needed to make decisions that please You.

Protect us and our families wherever our feet go this week. We look forward to meeting with You next holy Sabbath day.

In Jesus' name. Amen.

Fifth Sabbath Day

Let's enter into His presence with a word of prayer:

Heavenly Father,

Abide with us on this special day as we bless Your holy name in joyful worship. Forgive all the areas we have fallen short so we can be renewed and freely enter into Your presence—remembering Your beautiful creation, with family and friends gratefully assembled, bless us to enjoy each other as we celebrate. As we seek opportunities to plant seeds, may our keeping of the Sabbath day create curiosity and guide others into valuing this time and honoring You. Graciously entering into this time...

In Jesus' name. Amen!

Happy 5th Sabbath Day!

Journal Entry: I feel deeply humbled and refreshed more each Sabbath — profound learning and reflection. The desire within me to gain knowledge seems unquenchable. Even after Saturday's sundowns, I find myself reluctant to let go of the Sabbath rest and each Sabbath day brings more things I want to study. This Sabbath I did a study on **ancient biblical context** and was struck by the **danger of plucking a single verse to create a doctrine**. It's essential to see the entire story to grasp the concept of every message—not just the verse, but the whole chapter, and indeed, the entire book, encompassing both the Old and New Testaments.

Exploring history and ancient perceptions has been eye-opening for me, illuminating the Word in new ways. I recommend everyone learn more about ancient biblical writings, the way they talked, lived, and expressed themselves. It definitely brings a clearer understanding to us today. I find myself still on a quest for truth, yet simultaneously never wanting to cease in this pursuit. In all reality, as long as we are alive, we will have more truth to learn...

Truth Revealed: Guiding Generations

...and wow do I have a lot to learn. Changing 55 years of indoctrination is not only the craziest transformation but the most beautiful. Once you see the truth you cannot unsee it, am I right? :)

Now I am very careful to have scripture to back up anything I say to anyone, especially to my 4 children — raising them in church, thinking I was leading them down the right path and now they are adults and I can't remold their beliefs at this point, not like when they were under my roof, anyway.

Salysia, my oldest daughter, Jarrod, my firstborn son, and the twins, Jordan (my second son) and Samarah (my youngest daughter), have walked my spiritual journey with me. I feel a strong need to seek God's forgiveness for inadvertently sharing teachings that weren't based on my own understanding of Scripture or time spent with God. Rather, these were doctrines I had accepted without thorough verification from the Word. It's now clear to me how such misunderstandings can persist through generations.

Five weeks into this journey, I started discussing my Sabbath observance with Salysia and she received it without any problem. She trusts me when it comes to matters of God, and I am thankful to Him for keeping her heart open, willing even to explore scripture with me—a true blessing. Samarah, while she finishes out her college year, is still living at home with me and therefore her days are filled with Bible studies, music always playing in the background, and has been observing me keeping the Sabbath. Currently, she has not participated in the Sabbath herself, but she has no problem serving as an accountability partner, often asking humorously, "Mom, are you supposed to do that on the Sabbath?" She keeps a close eye on me :). I've also noticed her biblical knowledge has increased simply by having scriptures constantly in her ears — whether she listens subconsciously or consciously, she can answer biblical questions better than before.

My boys, Jarrod and Jordan, have strong, confident characters and have always been outspoken about their beliefs in God. Jarrod never had issues with bravery; boldly sharing his beliefs has never been a problem. Jordan, on the other hand, often expresses obedience about staying true to God. He is careful to ask for forgiveness and expresses gratitude for all things. So, while my children may not be experiencing their faith journey in the same way I am right now, I am incredibly blessed by the strong foundation they have. It brings me comfort and joy.

Update As I write this memoir, about 9 months after I celebrated the 5th Sabbath day, I see my children growing in their understanding of the truth. We now have family Bible studies via Zoom, including grandchildren—what a blessing for our spiritual growth. I am profoundly thankful to our Father for orchestrating this for us. I recognized that I couldn't change my children; they are grown now. Yet, their humble hearts remain open and because of that, our Father can reveal His truth. Hopefully, in the near future, we will be enjoying a Shabbat meal together.

I know there are many of you out there who have found the truth later on in life, as I do, and we worry about our families. Be reassured that they are watching you like everyone else, we can only plant seeds and as we all are coming to realize, God will open their eyes when He sees fit.

The Vine and The Branches

Even though we might just be coming to this truth does that mean we weren't in the truth before? We were doing the best we could for what we knew. Yes, it's our responsibility to read and learn for ourselves, but we also have to realize in our hearts we believed we were okay. A relationship with the Almighty is an ongoing journey and this new truth doesn't change that at all.

However, I do believe it should **produce good fruits**, for people to witness and then hopefully come to Him.

Matthew 7:15-20

"Watch out for false prophets. They come to you in sheep's clothing, but inwardly they are ferocious wolves. By their fruit you will recognize them. Do people pick grapes from thorn bushes, or figs from thistles? <u>Likewise, every good tree bears good fruit, but a bad tree bears bad fruit.</u> A good tree cannot bear bad fruit, and a bad tree cannot bear good fruit. Every tree that does not bear good fruit is cut down and thrown into the fire. Thus, by their fruit you will recognize them."

In these verses, Jesus warns about false prophets and emphasizes the importance of discerning their true nature by observing the fruit of their lives—meaning their actions, teachings, and the outcomes of their ministry. He uses the analogy of trees and fruit to illustrate that genuine followers of God will produce good fruit, while false prophets will produce bad fruit. This teaching underscores the significance of character and integrity in spiritual leadership and encourages discernment among believers.

This verse is part of Jesus's teaching about recognizing false prophets by their actions or "fruits." It emphasizes the idea that a person's character and true nature are revealed by the outcomes or results of their words and deeds

Bearing Good Fruit - The Evidence of Abiding in Him

It's a continual learning process and we should show more from it, not less. We are created by a God that loves us and as long as we are **abiding and remaining** in Him, He will guide us to Him fully. Many translations hold the same context, as seen below:

John 15:4

(KJV): "Abide in me, and I in you. As the branch cannot bear fruit of itself, except it abide in the vine; no more can ye, except ye abide in me."

(NLT): "Remain in me, and I will remain in you. For a branch cannot produce fruit if it is severed from the vine, and you cannot be fruitful unless you remain in me."

(TS2009): "Stay in Me, and I stay in you. As the branch is unable to bear fruit of itself, unless it stays in the vine, so neither you, unless you stay in Me

In all 3 translations, the message is clear.

- **Abide**: It means to stay, continue in a place, or to endure or tolerate something.

- **Remain**: It means to stay in the same place or condition, to continue to exist or be left after others are gone.

- **Stay:** It means to remain in a particular place, condition, or situation without moving away or to continue to be in a specified state or position. It implies a sense of continuity, persistence, or remaining in place over time.

In all 3 translations, whether it be, abide, remain, or stay, they are verbs used to convey the idea of **constantly staying connected, in a close relationship with Jesus, similar to how a branch stays connected to a vine to bear fruit.**

There is so much in John 15 — the entire chapter is Jesus speaking - let's take a look.

John 15 (The Scriptures)

"I am the true vine, and My Father is the gardener. Every branch in Me that bears no fruit He takes away. And every branch that bears fruit He prunes, so that

it bears more fruit. You are already clean because of
the Word which I have spoken to you. Stay in Me, and
I stay in you. As the branch is unable to bear fruit
of itself, unless it stays in the vine, so neither you,
unless you stay in Me.

I am the vine, you are the branches. He who stays
in Me, and I in him, he bears much fruit. Because
without Me you are able to do naught! If anyone does
not stay in Me, he is thrown away as a branch and
dries up. And they gather them and throw them into
the fire, and they are burned. If you stay in Me, and
My Words stay in you, you shall ask whatever you
wish, and it shall be done for you.

In this My Father is esteemed, that you bear much
fruit, and you shall be My taught ones. As the Father
has loved Me, I have also loved you. Stay in My love.
If you guard My commands, you shall stay in My love,
just as I have guarded My Father's commands and
stay in His love. These words I have spoken to you, so
that My joy might be in you, and that your joy might
be complete.

This is My command, that you love one another, as
I have loved you. No one has greater love than this:
that one should lay down his life for his friends. You
are My friends if you do whatever I command you.

No longer do I call you servants, for a servant does not know what his master is doing. But I have called you friends, for all teachings which I heard from My Father I have made known to you.

You did not choose Me, but I chose you and appointed you that you should go and bear fruit, and that your fruit should remain, so that whatever you ask the Father in My Name He might give you. These words I command you, so that you love one another. If the world hates you, you know that it hated Me before you. If you were of the world, the world would love its own. But because you are not of the world, but I chose you out of the world, for that reason the world hates you.

Remember the word that I said to you, 'A servant is not greater than his master.' If they persecuted Me, they shall persecute you too. If they have guarded My Word, they would guard yours too. But all this they shall do to you because of My Name, because they do not know Him who sent Me. If I had not come and spoken to them, they would have no sin, but now they have no excuse for their sin.

He who hates Me hates My Father as well. If I did not do among them the works which no one else did, they would have no sin. But now they have both seen

and have hated both Me and My Father. But that the word might be filled which was written in their Torah, 'They hated Me without a cause.' And when the Helper comes, whom I shall send to you from the Father, the Spirit of the Truth, who comes from the Father, He shall bear witness of Me, but you also bear witness, because you have been with Me from the beginning."

The chapter John 15 in the Bible holds several key teachings and meanings conveyed by Jesus:

1. **Jesus as the True Vine**: Jesus uses the metaphor of Himself as the true vine, and His disciples as the branches. This illustrates the intimate and necessary connection believers must maintain with Him to bear spiritual fruit. Just as branches draw their life and sustenance from the vine, so too must disciples remain connected to Jesus to experience spiritual growth and effectiveness in their lives.

2. **Abiding in Jesus**: The concept of "abiding" is central to this chapter. Jesus emphasizes the need for His followers to remain in Him, which involves staying close to Him in faith, obedience, and relationship. This abiding is not

just a passive state but involves active trust, obedience to His teachings, and a continual dependence on His presence and power.

3. **Bearing Fruit**: Jesus teaches that those who abide in Him will bear much fruit. This fruit refers to the qualities of a Christlike life—love, joy, peace, patience, kindness, goodness, faithfulness, gentleness, and self-control (Galatians 5:22-23)—as well as the good works and influences that result from living out faith in Him. The fruitfulness of the branches (disciples) is evidence of their connection to the vine (Jesus).

4. **Love and Obedience**: Jesus stresses the importance of love, both His love for His disciples and their love for one another. He commands them to love one another as He has loved them, which includes sacrificial love and service. Obedience to His commands is a natural outflow of abiding in His love and results in a life that glorifies God and reflects His character.

5. **Promise of the Holy Spirit**: Jesus promises the coming of the Holy Spirit, the Advocate,

who will empower and guide His followers. The Spirit will testify about Jesus and enable believers to bear witness to Him effectively.

6. **Expectation of Persecution**: Jesus warns His disciples that the world will oppose them because of their association with Him. They should expect persecution and hatred, similar to what Jesus Himself experienced. This persecution serves as a reminder of their distinct identity as followers of Christ and the contrast between the values of the kingdom of God and the world.

In summary, John 15 conveys Jesus's teachings on the vital importance of remaining in Him, bearing fruit through love and obedience, and the empowering presence of the Holy Spirit. It underscores the transformative relationship believers have with Jesus, emphasizing a life of faithfulness, fruitfulness, and enduring in the face of opposition.

If you noticed, I highlighted a part of John, Chapter 15: **If you guard My commands, you shall stay in My love, just as I have guarded My Father's commands and stay in His love.** "Guard the commands" is a very important statement to remember. I will talk more about this in an upcoming chapter, but for now, think about Jesus's instructions here and the promise He will keep to us if we follow those instructions.

As the 5th Sabbath day closes, let's pray:

Father,

Thank you for a special time with You, family, and friends. What an honor to be part of the day You created and set apart for us. You are worthy to be praised for eternity without ceasing.

Bless us with Your guidance and protection as we venture out into the world this week. As we open the Word throughout the following days, give us the ability to understand Your truth. Truth found in Your Word, through You and only You. As we share scripture with others, keep our hearts humbled and remind us that we need to teach lovingly and not full of pride.

We ask for the gift of discernment so when talking to others about You we only speak Your truths as we do not want to spread untruths.

Protect us and our families over the next week as we anticipate meeting with You every day, and especially next Friday at dusk. Praises to You, the Most High.

In Jesus' name. Amen!

Sixth Sabbath Day

Let's begin this beautiful night with a prayer:

Creator of Heaven and Earth,

How we love you so. You indeed crafted this day for us, for all of mankind, to revel in Your glory fully and without interruption, forging a bond with You that we cherish more with each passing moment as the Friday sunsets. You are worthy of all our praises and devotion. We serve you gladly and gratefully, oh Lord. As we enter into this sacred time with you once again, a time set apart for your children, we humbly ask for your forgiveness for any shortcomings or transgressions. Cleanse our hearts and minds, so we may enter into your divine presence with hearts wide open. Reveal to us your truths and shower us with your love.

In Jesus' name, amen

Stillness in Dusk's Awakening

Journal Entry: As the sun gracefully retreats beyond the horizon, twilight envelops the world in its gentle embrace. That fleeting moment, when day and night converge, holds a magic of its own. The sky blushes with hues of lavender and rose, and the air grows hushed as if the universe itself takes a breath.

In this tranquil moment, I find solace—a pause to reflect on the day's endeavors, the challenges met, and the joys experienced. The symphony of existence quiets, allowing our souls to resonate with gratitude. Even as the sun departs, it leaves behind a legacy of light and warmth.

I welcome the Sabbath with an open heart, as the stars emerge one by one, stitching constellations across the canvas of the night. May this sacred time bring renewal, connection, and serenity to my spirit.

The notifications on my devices now rest in silence — a digital Sabbath of their own.

I would say everyone in my circle has figured out and accepted that I will not be available until Saturday night. I am grateful for the floods of texts that came through in the last daylight hour on Friday. 'Have a good Sabbath!' they chime. 'Call me after your

Sabbath.' 'Try to call me before your Sabbath.' 'Are you keeping the Sabbath?' Their concern, once confused, now urgently trying to connect before the 24 hours I 'go missing.' LOL! It's only 24 hours; I'm only at home resting. I'm not leaving on a world tour. Maybe their curiosity is heightened, and they feel like they are missing out on something. If so, they know they are more than welcome to participate in the Sabbath with me. :)

Reflections of Our Journey

Have you realized we've been enjoying our holy days for over a month now? Do the weeks fly by for you too? By Wednesday, do you find yourself eagerly anticipating Sabbath day, longing for the restful celebration to begin? I know I do, my mind and body know.

Are you feeling a sense of separation from your friends, family, or community? I hope this hasn't happened to you, but I have experienced it, even if only in small amounts. Some may try to make you feel as though you're acting irrationally but don't give up on what God has called you to do. You might feel very alone, especially if there are no Sabbath-keeping groups in your area. This is another reason why I feel led to write this book—it connects me to you. Brothers and sisters, even though we haven't met and you may feel like fictional characters in my story right now, I know in spirit that God is preparing your hearts as I type these words.

We might never understand why some people respond the way they do when we mention that we're observing the Sabbath. Some will announce, "We aren't under that covenant anymore," and some even go so far as to preach that we don't have to keep the commandments. Honestly, it scares me to think that Jesus's death didn't establish any standard at all—it's been weighing on me.

I believe it's crucial for church leaders to ensure that the congregation truly understands the Bible. It's not just about flashing a verse on a screen and then filling the time with unrelated topics. When we gather, there's a real opportunity for deep, meaningful study that brings knowledge. Teach us the etymology of the words, the history, the context... We should leave church feeling equipped as if we've been in a classroom where the Scriptures come alive with understanding. It's about more than just surface-level engagement; it's about fostering a deep connection with God and a clear understanding of the Word.

So many denominations exist — somewhere around 40,000 — and everyone believes in a different doctrine. How can this be? There are those who claim to follow the commandments but just not the fourth one. Is it okay to pick and choose — to toss out a commandment? Then, there are those who say they believe we should keep the Sabbath, but they choose their own day to rest. It's mind-boggling! So, you get to decide if you want to follow the rules if you want to keep all ten, and if you want to apply them only when you feel like it? What is going on?! Catholics have a bad rap, but all I see are little spin-offs of Catholicism. They change one tiny thing they don't like or don't believe, but the foundation really doesn't change: pagan holidays like Easter and Christmas—no feasts, no Sabbaths...

Emulation of Catholic Practices

In our contemporary denominations, despite their divergent doctrinal paths, there exists an intriguing continuity — a genetic thread connecting them back to the theological DNA of Roman Catholicism across generations. Remarkably, even within traditions that vocally oppose Catholicism, subtle echoes of those ancient ideological frameworks persist. So, to all the people stuck in one of the 40,000-plus denominations who think so poorly of "the Catholics," you are, in fact, Catholic. Your denomination is a spin-off — All roads lead to Rome!

Christianization of Pagan Practices

As Christianity became the official religion of the Roman Empire in the 4th century under Emperor Constantine, efforts were made to Christianize pagan practices and festivals to facilitate the conversion of pagan populations. This process sometimes involved adapting or replacing existing pagan holidays with Christian celebrations, such as Christmas and Easter, which absorbed elements of pre-existing pagan festivals.

Christianity faced the question of how to integrate Gentile (non-Jewish) converts into a predominantly Jewish movement. The apostolic council decided that Gentile believers did not need to observe Jewish ceremonial laws, including circumcision and dietary restrictions, as a requirement for salvation. This decision set a precedent for the differentiation between Jewish and Gentile practices within early Christianity.

How convenient that the Roman Empire excludes the entire Jewish culture under the disguise of Baptist,

Protestant, Non-denominational...whatever Christian spin-off you're in. It has done away with what we are called to be — **set apart**! Before we criticize the Catholics, we might want to ask ourselves if we're embodying the very practices we reject.

I do believe our steady faithfulness in honoring this Sabbath gift, though feeling peculiar for now, carves a path to walk new directions beyond religious institutions. **Let's be set apart together! Let us follow the _Way_.**

John 14:6

"Jesus saith unto him, 'I am the _way_, the truth, and the life: no man cometh unto the Father, but by me.'"

This verse emphasizes Jesus as "the Way" in the context of salvation and following His teachings.

Sabbath Mornings and Coffee

Journal Entry: Good morning, Saturday! What a wonderful Friday evening spent worshiping and studying the Lord's word. A few weeks ago, I wasn't even sure of the Sabbath rules — could I go to the beach or out anywhere for that matter? I have learned that it is recommended, especially on this particular day, to celebrate all of His creation. What better way to do that than by walking on the beach, hiking through the woods, riding a bike, laying in a park with a good book, or sitting on a porch swing listening to worship music—maybe even strolling down a city street with a coffee you made at home in a Yeti cup, of course.

As for today, the beach is calling. I love when a morning low tide lines up with a walk. Everything is flat, and there is much more beach to choose from. :). As I walk along trying to dodge jellyfish and shells while keeping my feet in the water, it almost feels like I'm a little kid again. There's something about kicking the water as I go — it makes me feel so free and thankful to be standing in such a beautiful, amazing place. The sun is warm on my skin, and the sound of waves crashing in the distance is both soothing and exhilarating. Each step I take leaves a temporary imprint in the wet sand, a reminder of my small presence in this vast, timeless expanse, humbly creating a perspective of how little time we have to achieve what we need.

I pause for a moment to pick up a smooth, weathered shell, marveling at its intricate patterns. I think it relates very well to what we are doing here, being smoothed out by our love and convictions making us uniquely beautiful. We all know it won't come without persecution, trials and tribulations.

James 1:2-4

"Consider it pure joy, my brothers and sisters, whenever you face trials of many kinds, because you know that the testing of your faith produces perseverance. Let perseverance finish its work so that you may be mature and complete, not lacking anything."

Matthew 5:10

"Blessed are those who are persecuted for righteousness' sake, for theirs is the kingdom of heaven."

For me, it is a learning process to experience a trial and walk through it with little concern because you know that God is taking care of it. I still struggle with this today.

I believe we all understand we are called to be set apart and **to be in this world but not of this world...**

In The World but Not Of The World

John 17:14-16

"I have given them your word, and the world has hated them, for they are not of the world any more than I am of the world. My prayer is not that you take them out of the world but that you protect them from the evil one. They are not of the world, even as I am not of it."

In this passage, Jesus prays to God the Father about his disciples before his crucifixion. He acknowledges that although his followers must remain physically present in the world, they do not share sinful values and desires.

Through faith and obedience to God's word, believers can remain spiritually pure and set apart, even while interacting with those who live worldly lifestyles. The goal is to align with God rather than compromise under pressure from ungodly cultural influences.

While followers of Christ must function in the world, they should not adopt selfish mindsets or sinful behaviors. Their primary identity is now tied to Jesus and the Kingdom of Heaven rather than the flawed values of the fallen world.

Several Old Testament verses connect the concept of being **set apart or holy by keeping the Sabbath:**

Exodus 31:13

"Verily my sabbaths ye shall keep: for it is a sign between me and you throughout your generations; that ye may know that I am the LORD that doth sanctify you."

The Sabbath serves as a sign of a unique relationship with our Father. By dedicating this day to God, we demonstrate commitment to love, serve, and obey Him. It signifies who we belong to.

Ezekiel 20:12

"Moreover I also gave them my Sabbath, to be a sign between me and them, that they might know that I am the LORD that sanctifies them."

Ezekiel 20:20:

"And hallow my sabbaths; and they shall be a sign between me and you, that ye may know that I am the LORD your God."

Again, here are passages emphasizing that keeping the Sabbath holy is a visible sign of God's people being set apart. It reminds us that He alone sanctifies us as we walk in covenant obedience. The weekly Sabbaths signify our special consecration to the Creator.

Let's close out this sabbath day with thanksgiving:

Dear God,

We have many things we can thank You for this evening. The way You are opening up truth and relationship with You is the most cherished time of our week.

To be set apart from the world but to be connected to You through love and obedience holds many blessings. We are eternally grateful — You, who began a good work in us, have never stopped showing up to meet us where we are.

As Your word says in Philippians 1:6 "For I am confident of this very thing, that He who began a good work in you will perfect it until the day of Christ Jesus."

Bless each and every one of us here tonight and protect us and our families as we head into this week.

All praises to You, our Most High!

In Jesus' name. Amen!

Seventh Sabbath Day

As we begin:

Heavenly Father,

As we come before you clear our hearts and our minds from this week's responsibilities and worries. Let us feel renewed and focus on all the blessings you've given us throughout our lives. You are worthy to be praised, Father. We love you and let this time spent with you bring You honor and glory- for all good things are from you.

In His precious name. Amen

Sabbaths and Stormy Sunsets

Journal Entry: As Friday's sunset approaches, I'm filled with overwhelming joy, eagerly anticipating the Sabbath. It feels extra comfy cozy tonight as a storm is brewing outside, which sets a mood of slumber and ambiance. As the wind howls outside and rain beats against the windows, I light candles, pour myself a glass of wine, and settle into my studies.

I always know there's a world of online Sabbath hosts that go live, offering opportunities for fellowship and learning—unless we lose power and WiFi, of course.

It's been only seven weeks since we've been meeting here, and I think I can safely say we've all been on a super-fast crash course in truth. It's been a journey for the books (get it...I'm writing this book...okay, moving on...), for sure. I know we all faced a lot of questions, but as quickly as the chaos came and went, those who are closest are coming around. They are accepting, and some are starting to see the truth along with us.

It is very possible you all have found someone close who wants to start hearing about your Sabbath adventure, maybe even interested in honoring one. This blessing is catchy, isn't it, brothers and sisters? Praises to the Most High...always!

I have been thoroughly enjoying time with my oldest daughter, a mother herself, who is eager to understand why I honor the Sabbath. Together, we delve into scripture, and witnessing her newfound understanding fills me with profound joy. She gets so excited when she finds scripture nuggets — small but precious bits of truth.

One thing for sure is that I am grateful for the changes I see in myself and the rapid growth of my knowledge of His word on these Sabbath days. I'm also grateful for my newfound love for the commandments. I never thought of them as often as I do now, and they are the guidelines set for me to please my Father. I have learned that I am sinning more than I thought, and realizing that allowed me to work towards a more righteous life in Him. If everyone would just honor ONE Sabbath day, they would understand the blessings! Do you agree, brothers and sisters?

Sabbaths and Sunny Sunrises

Journal Entry: Saturday morning sunrays are shining through the curtains; another storm has passed by, and a glorious day begins. Hallelujah!

Saturday turned out to be glorious. I spent some time with family on a nearby island, roaming around in a golf cart. Looking at the ocean on a Sabbath day makes it a little bit more special to me—so peaceful.

It's not a secret, as you all know by now, that I love the ocean views; I love the beach, **but** spending a day on it with my sisters means the world to me. Just being with them is like opening a time capsule—familiar scenery, family, scents, food — it is bringing it all back.

From childhood to adulthood, the East Coast has been a constant presence in my life—a source of solace, inspiration, and endless wonder. I grew up in a blessed place on the coast of Massachusetts, about 5 minutes from the New Hampshire border and minutes from the Maine border. Roaming all three states in one day was common for us growing up. The woods and mountains of New Hampshire, and the lakes, parks, and lighthouses of Maine; are just beautiful. There's only one reason a girl moves away from there and goes south—no snow! Sure, it's beautiful, but it's a very difficult climate to live in. I have the best of three worlds: a house on the southern coastline, nestled in the thick of the woods, and a family up north I can visit when I miss the snow.

The school year was spent in the city, and the summers were at the beach house. I can still recall the excitement that bubbled within me as my parents packed the car on our last day of school to spend the summer at the beach. The anticipation was palpable as we saw all the local beach restaurants in view, and then that giant whale—some monument—and the smell of salty air meant we were now at the beach.

With towels and drinks in hand, my siblings, cousins, and I would spend hours with our feet in the sand, riding the waves, and walking to The Center, as we called it. Walks to The Center to buy German fries with vinegar at the request of many aunts and uncles, and oh, that beach pizza, "a slice of provolone on that, please." If you know, you know—'beach pizza.' Aunts and uncles playing cards while we built bonfires and cousins all around made it a constant celebration.

To this day, I wander along the shores, lost in thought as I watch the waves crash, but now I see mostly pelicans instead of seagulls. The ocean now is warm compared to the ice-cold New England waters. The vastness of the ocean mirrors the memory, feel, and smell of my childhood. Even when the uncertainty of my future is present, the ocean stores all my memories and makes hope and happiness possible — always. It's a consistent, constant love, much like the feeling when I think of the Father—you can always count on that sense of peace and certainty.

I wish I could hear about the favorite memories you had as a child and I know I am making my childhood look like a basket of candy and rainbows but it wasn't. I am focusing now on the good things I can recall that made it special. Just like our lives now, we have hardships but we can pull out the goodness — what God has done for us!

Fun Facts: The Perfect Number 7

Since this is Chapter 7, it seems fitting to highlight the significance of the number 7 in the Bible, which represents perfection, completion, and much more. This chapter dedicates itself to exploring the number 7 because of its profound meaning and its frequent occurrence in scripture. When our Creator instructs us to "keep the 7th day holy," it underscores the importance of this number in His divine plan. Numbers, days, appointments, and times hold great significance for Him, and understanding the meaning of the number 7 can deepen our appreciation of its role in our spiritual journey.

God **created** the world in six days and rested on the seventh, establishing the Sabbath.

The **Sabbath** serves as a day of rest and reflection for believers on **day 7**.

Farmers were instructed to let their **fields** rest every **seventh year** (Leviticus 25:2-4).

The **seven-day week** is a standard rooted in ancient civilizations and remains relevant today.

The **rainbow**, a biblical symbol of promise, contains seven colors, further underscoring the beauty and significance of the number.

The seven-branched **menorah** in the Temple represents divine light and wisdom, highlighting the sacredness of the number seven in Jewish tradition.

God established **seven feasts** in Leviticus 23, commemorating key events in Israel's history.

The prophecy of **seventy weeks** in Daniel signifies important eschatological timelines.

In Revelation, Jesus addresses **seven churches**, representing the completeness of the church's messages.

The opening of the **seven seals** in Revelation signifies God's plan and judgment.

Each of the **seven trumpets** in the book of Revelation serves as a crucial step in the unfolding of God's plan, culminating in the establishment of His Kingdom and the ultimate restoration of creation.

These **seven bowls** in the book of Revelation contain God's final judgments poured out upon the earth, representing the culmination of His wrath against sin and evil.

The Israelites **marched seven times** around Jericho, demonstrating God's power through obedience.

Proverbs 9:1 describes wisdom as having **seven pillars**, symbolizing strength and stability. Understanding, knowledge, counsel, strength, righteousness, judgment, and fear of the Lord.

Jesus spoke **seven phrases** while crucified, each rich in meaning.

1. "Father, forgive them; for they know not what they do."

2. "Verily I say unto thee, Today shalt thou be with me in paradise."

3. "Woman, behold thy son! ... Behold thy mother!"

4. "My God, my God, why hast thou forsaken me?"

5. "I thirst."

6. "It is finished."

7. "Father, into thy hands I commend my spirit."

Seals, Trumpets and Bowls — Oh My!

Seven Seals

1. The first seal reveals a rider on a white horse, symbolizing conquest (Revelation 6:1-2).

2. The second seal brings a rider on a red horse, representing war and bloodshed (Revelation 6:3-4).

3. The third seal features a rider on a black horse, signifying famine (Revelation 6:5-6).

4. The fourth seal shows a pale horse, whose rider is Death (Revelation 6:7-8).

5. The fifth seal reveals the souls of martyrs under the altar, crying out for justice (Revelation 6:9-11).

6. The sixth seal unleashes cosmic disturbances, including earthquakes and the darkening of the sun (Revelation 6:12-17).

7. The seventh seal leads to silence in heaven and introduces the seven trumpets (Revelation 8:1).

Seven Trumpets

1. The first trumpet brings hail and fire mixed with blood, burning a third of the earth (Revelation 8:7).

2. The second trumpet causes a great mountain burning with fire to be thrown into the sea, turning a third of the sea into blood (Revelation 8:8-9).

3. The third trumpet introduces a star called Wormwood, poisoning a third of the rivers and springs (Revelation 8:10-11).

4. The fourth trumpet darkens a third of the sun, moon, and stars (Revelation 8:12).

5. The fifth trumpet releases locusts from the abyss to torment those without the seal of God (Revelation 9:1-11).

6. The sixth trumpet brings the release of four angels who kill a third of mankind (Revelation 9:13-21).

7. The seventh trumpet proclaims the kingdom of God and initiates final judgments (Revelation 11:15-19).

Seven Bowls

1. The first bowl causes painful sores to afflict those who have the mark of the beast (Revelation 16:2).

2. The second bowl turns the sea into blood, killing all living things (Revelation 16:3).

3. The third bowl makes the rivers and springs blood, signifying judgment on those who shed the blood of the saints (Revelation 16:4-7).

4. The fourth bowl scorches people with intense heat from the sun (Revelation 16:8-9).

5. The fifth bowl brings darkness upon the kingdom of the beast, leading to great suffering (Revelation 16:10-11).

6. The sixth bowl dries up the Euphrates River, preparing the way for the kings of the east and gathering demonic spirits for battle (Revelation 16:12-16).

7. The seventh bowl results in a great earthquake and hailstones, marking the completion of God's judgment (Revelation 16:17-21).

God of Numbers

God is a God of numbers and order. Throughout the Bible, numbers like **12** symbolize God's people, as seen in the apostles, tribes, and the New Jerusalem temple gates. Then the number **40**, often associated with testing and preparation, such as the flood, living in the wilderness, and Jesus's fasting and temptation in the desert-hold significant meaning. Each number reflects God's divine plan and purpose.

Given the significance that numbers hold in Scripture, it is essential for us to recognize the importance of the 7th day. If God gives us a specific number, it signifies His order and intention for our lives. The 7th day Sabbath is a powerful reminder that we should align ourselves with the divine structure He has established. Ignoring or underestimating the significance of this number may lead us to miss out on the fullness of what God has intended for us.

Let's close this day with a prayer:

Heavenly Father, Creator of all things,

Our hearts overflow with gratitude as we continue to journey in truth and connection with You.

With each passing day, our love for You deepens, and our bond with You strengthens in ways we never imagined.

We are humbled by Your endless grace and mercy, which welcomes us into Your presence regardless of when we arrive. Like the prodigal son, like the thief on the cross, like the laborers in the vineyard, You embrace us with open arms, showering us with Your blessings and love.

As we navigate the challenges of each passing week, help us to remain steadfast in our faith and trust in Your sovereign control over all things. Remind us that our time with You, our Sabbath rest draws near and in Your presence, we find peace and renewal. Grant us the wisdom and strength to persevere through life's trials, knowing that You are always with us, guiding and sustaining us.

In the name of our Messiah, we pray. Amen.

Eighth Sabbath Day

As we enter into His holy day, let's pray:

Father God,

As we approach Your presence tonight, may You remind us that You are the reason we have all come together, united in praise. Since the beginning of time, You have set this day apart for rest and therefore set us apart from the world. Already we thank You for the nourishment You provided for our bodies and the ability to prepare meals and sit at Your spiritual table weekly. As we study Your name, guide us to the truths in Scripture, as only You can do. Our goal is to live by Your truth, not the world's truths, for Yours alone sets us free.

We pray this in the saving name of Jesus. Amen!

Notifications Off, Silence On

Journal Entry: Hello my friends. Who here cannot wait to shut their phones off? I'm actually at the point where on Saturday night, I dread turning all my notifications back on. It's like a full-time job catching up with all the emails, texts, calls, Facebook, Instagram, Snapchat.... The stress just floods back.

In the tranquil serenity of my home, I've become adept at crafting the perfect ambiance: flickering candles casting a warm glow, plush throw pillows and blankets inviting relaxation. The electric tea pot stands ready, stocked with an array of different teas to suit any preference.

As the soothing strains of worship music fill the air, my faithful companion Zeke curls up beside me, surrendering to sleep.

Tonight and into tomorrow, I'll delve into research and participate in my live Bible studies, and I already can feel a nap coming on for tomorrow. There's a sense of anticipation, a feeling that this time spent in study may lead us to explore new names for our divine Creator. Only time will tell.

Rabbit Holes: Do They Have An End

As the sun descends, the Sabbath begins. But... does it? When does the 'day' end? When does it begin? Does the biblical day start at sunset or sunrise? Is the Sabbath day 24 hours or is it just 12 hours, the daytime, the hours of light? Does it start on Friday sunset or Saturday sunrise? I guess one comforting thing for sure is we all are honoring it on Saturday during the day.

But wait again...ready for this tailspin? Let's add to the confusion and let me ask you if it is actually on Saturday? When were the 'day names' invented? The 7-day week in Genesis does not have names assigned, just the number of the day. Day 2 follows day 1.... So why Saturday? Where does the name Saturday come from, and how do we know for sure it's the original 7th day?

Another monkey wrench, The Book of Enoch. This book is part of the apocrypha which takes us off topic a bit but I must mention it. If you believe in the apocrypha then you have to take Enoch into account when learning about the Sabbath day. I personally take Enoch's book into account for the following reasons:

-Enoch is mentioned in the Bible we read.

-The book of Enoch was taken out of the bible (very sus)

-The book of Enoch was found in the Dead Sea Scrolls

If you do take Enoch seriously, there is a lot to learn about the days and seasons, and the way he teaches how to follow these times. From what I am currently understanding, he uses the sun, equinoxes, and a 364-day year cycle. I am giving you an extremely basic summary about Enoch — I am not qualified, in the slightest, to teach it at any level, just giving you enough so you know there are people who follow Enoch and his portals to tell time. In my opinion, I have to say it is detailed and could be possible. If you come to believe Enoch's teaching you will find that the Sabbath day is different each year after the equinox (the biblical new year). The Enoch way is what I am studying as I type this sentence, but I haven't completely concluded.

As you can gather, I have come across this topic several times in my 'new to truth' journey which has not been very long. I have been diligently studying this, and thus far, I haven't found 100% clarity to change my ways. As I am writing this memoir (11 months after my 8th-week journal entry was written) I have not found the answer. Maybe I am correctly honoring it and that's why I haven't found an absolute. I can see scripture matching other's points of view clearly, and there is truth in the discussions that leads me to continue seeking and praying for His truth to be revealed to me. If you are in the same place as me, permit yourself to be okay with the time it takes for our Father to reveal it to you. Some periods we are given truths in tiny crumbs, and other times we are fed a buffet in one sitting. I know you know we cannot question His strategy for us, but we all do know He has our best interest in mind.

To elaborate, my current conclusion is Friday sunset to Saturday sunset.

Nehemiah 13:19

"So it was, at the gates of Jerusalem, as it began to be dark before the Sabbath, that I commanded the gates to be shut, and charged that they must not be opened till after the Sabbath. Then I posted some of my servants at the gates, so that no burdens would be brought in on the Sabbath day."

From the time of Nehemiah (around 445 BCE) to Jesus (around 30 CE), Sabbath observance among the Jewish people remained consistent, observed from evening to evening. However, based on that verse, I cannot definitively confirm that it was from Friday to Saturday. Since the days of the week had names when the Messiah walked among us, I assume it must have been Friday to Saturday, as it is now. Later, Constantine declared Sunday as the first day of the week, which again points to Saturday as the seventh day but who at this point believes anything Constantine declares? Not me! He could be the one Daniel talks about in 7:25 "He will speak against the Most High and oppress his holy people and try to change the set times and the laws. The holy people will be delivered into his hands for a time, times, and half a time."

Obviously, more studying has to be conducted on this topic and I am sure some of you are settled on the topic I pray I will get there too, soon!

Wavering vs Learning

To be really honest, it is so upsetting to me when I have confusion about His word. I wonder why I am not hearing Him and understanding His letter to me. It is scary to me to be wavering in my belief on any topic. We have to be kind to ourselves, allow grace, and understand we are ALL in the process of learning something new, and may that never change. As long as we live there are things to learn and we will still never have it all correct. It's why I will always want you to look into scripture yourself and find all the answers from Him.

Shabbat Shalom Family

Hello, tomorrow! It's Saturday morning and I've already found myself deep into a new rabbit hole. What is His true name? I've honestly done my best, but there are differing opinions, both for and against my conclusions. Everyone seems as certain about their findings as I am about mine.

Reflecting on these past weeks, I've delved into studying, researching, and learning more than ever before in my life. How about all of you?

I imagine you must be encountering revelations similar to mine, mostly doctrinal insights. Have you noticed people referring to God as Elohim, Yahweh-YHWH, Yahova-YHVH, Yahuah, and Yah?

I've seen Jesus called Yeshua, Iesous, Yahusha, Yahshua, Yahushua, Yeshua, and even Zeus. Of course, I have to check this out, don't we all? When some new information arises, aren't we called to check into it, and hear out the entire matter? In previous chapters, we talked about this, and I still believe we must look into the unknown, to some level, because we are not always right and there is always room for growth in truth. The

'Name Game' is a new topic to me and I am required to seek out the truth, show myself approved and work out my salvation, starting with questioning myself and why I say 'God' and 'Jesus.'

Honestly, I once thought I was okay to say God because I believe in only one God, so 'God' sufficed for me, just as 'Jesus' works, regardless of translations from Hebrew. I figured our Creator knows what I mean. Then someone asked me, 'How would you like it if I called you by a different name?' Trying to prove a point that we all want to be called by our real name, even the Father. That's all it took for me to embark on this new mission. What shall we call our Father and His Son?

Quick question, is it bad to be on a second pot of coffee by 11 a.m. and forget to eat because you're so consumed with the task at hand? This name search will be my focus on this Sabbath day.

His Name - In His Name

יהושע-יהוה

Navigating the Name of Our Creator

If last night's rabbit hole wasn't enough excitement for us, my quest to discover the true name of our Father and Messiah certainly took it to the next level. I had driven myself nearly insane searching for this truth. I often wondered whether the truth was truly elusive or if I was making it more complicated than it needed to be. But I pressed on to uncover what name to call our Father and Messiah.

This journey had been incredibly challenging. I wanted to know the truth so badly that my lack of confidence in my findings made me feel discouraged. It was maddening to the point of obsession. My focus on finding the correct names began to overshadow my conversations with my Father. Every time I prayed, I was preoccupied with how to address Him instead of simply speaking with Him.

I had become like a frantic child, determined to pass a test. Eventually, I realized that this obsession was consuming me—perhaps it was a distraction crafted by the enemy to divert my attention from what truly mattered. But even then, I questioned: What name should I actually use? Everyone seemed to have a strong opinion, each insisting that their preferred name was the correct one.

At one point, I decided to refer to Him as "Lord." However, someone kindly told me I couldn't use the name "Lord" because it also refers to Ba'al, a pagan god. What they left out is it also means "Master," which seemed perfectly appropriate since He is indeed our Master. People have used the term "Lord" to refer to kings and husbands—a title of respect and reverence. It was easy to get lost in these rules, but I learned that my Father loves me deeply and understands my heart. He is a parent of justice and mercy.

I learned to talk to my Father, trusting that He would guide me to a name that resonated with me. I also became frustrated because these debates had disrupted my natural communication with God and Jesus. It became clear to me that arguing over these matters was unacceptable.

To teachers, I urge you to remember to meet people where they are. Be kind and patient. Recall that you were once in their position. As new seekers of truth, we were overwhelmed with information we had never encountered before. Teachers should trust that God would do the work in us—guiding us gently, without resorting to fear-based techniques. It was unacceptable to argue about these matters. Many might abandon their newfound truth, mistaking it for legalism and rituals. I was grateful that I persisted, but some would not. They might walk away for good, and we did not want that on our hands.

When speaking to newcomers, I learned the importance of using familiar terms. Meeting them where they are in their walk reflected humility and truth—a principle I continue to follow. For instance, just eight weeks ago, my observance of the Sabbath shifted from non-existent to central in my walk with God. I would have loved for seasoned believers to join this discovery process so they could understand what newcomers like us faced. Seeing our perspective would better equip veterans to provide wise guidance.

Case in point - If a learned scholar had approached me eight weeks ago, rattling off "Yod He Vav He,"

"Yahovah," "Yahweh" or "Yahuah," I would have been completely baffled, thinking, "What in the world?"

Rant time — we must sensitively meet inquiring souls wherever they are, then lovingly guide them to a deeper understanding of God's names, doctrines, and nature through patient teaching. I had seen many times how less-experienced believers would ask a question, only to be overwhelmed with deep knowledge that took years to uncover. The responder often expected the newcomer to grasp it instantly, which usually pushed them away. Why would someone do that? Perhaps it was pride? They seemed eager to show off their knowledge the moment they got a chance. LET'S LOVE PEOPLE TO THE TRUTH! Rant over...

Yahuah

יהוה

Yah-hoo-ah

𐤅𐤄𐤅𐤉

The Father

The search for the Creator's and Messiah's true names has involved deep prayer, tears, and extensive research. While I feel confident in the names I've found, I remain open to new insights. I encourage you to explore and seek out this knowledge for yourself to find your own understanding and conclusion.

Understanding Etymology

Before we delve into the chapter on the Creator's name, it's helpful to understand **etymology**. Etymology is the study of the origin and historical development of words. It examines the root components of words, their meanings, and how they have evolved over time. This includes analyzing their linguistic ancestry, changes in form, and cultural and historical contexts. In our exploration, we will see how the **Tetragrammaton**—the four-letter name for the Creator—fits into this broader study of language and meaning.

Unveiling the Creator's Name

The search for the Creator's true name has captivated minds for generations. This chapter delves into the origins and significance of the name "**Yahuah**," revealing how it captures the essence of the Creator more fully than traditional renderings.

We'll explore why "**Yahuah**" is considered a more accurate representation of the Creator's name, especially in light of historical and linguistic factors that challenge the traditional "**Yahweh**" (YHWH) or "**Yahovah**" (YHVH).

Exploring the Creator's Name: Yahuah

As we dive deep into the study of the Creator's name, we encounter the **Tetragrammaton**—the four-letter name, **YHVH (Yod-He-Vav-He)**. This name is central to understanding the identity of the Creator and has been the subject of much debate and study over the centuries.

Pronunciation and the Vav Sound

In ancient Hebrew, the letter **Vav** was pronounced as double "**uu**" to sound like "**oo**." Over time, different methods were used to transliterate Hebrew letters into other alphabets. In some cases, the **Vav** was transliterated as "**W**," especially in Germanic languages, where "**W**" often represents a sound closer to "**V**" in English, which influenced the widespread use of "**YHWH**."

The use of "**YHWH**" or "**Yahweh**" became standardized in many English translations and theological writings, but some translations would use "**Vav**" as "**V**," resulting in "**YHVH**" or "**Yahovah**."

Why "Yahuah" Instead of "Yahovah or Yahweh"?

The pronunciation "**Yahuah**" versus "**Yahovah and Yahweh**" stems from how the Tetragrammaton is vocalized.

"**Yahuah**" reflects an attempt to reconstruct the pronunciation based on more ancient understandings, **avoiding the influence of later vowel insertions seen in "Yahovah and Yahweh."**

The "U" Sound in "Yahuah": The "**U**" sound in "**Yahuah**" is derived from other Hebrew names, such as **"Yahudah"** (**Judah**), where the **"U"** sound is present. This is thought to also preserve the original sounds (uu and oo) of the name more accurately.

The **"O"** sound in **"Yahovah"** is considered by some to be a later addition influenced by the Masoretes or by the **Latinized version "Jehovah,"** which is less accurate in reflecting the ancient pronunciation. Especially since the letter **"J"** didn't exist in the original Hebrew, Aramaic, or Greek texts of the Bible, it is a newer addition to English.

The use of "Yahuah" aims to align closely with the earliest and most authentic forms of the sacred name, reflecting the ancient pronunciation as accurately as possible. While **"YHWH"** or **"YHVH"** might be more familiar to many, **"Yahuah"** is believed to better preserve the original intent and sound of the Creator's name, keeping in line with the etymological and linguistic evidence.

The Tetragrammaton: The Four Letters That Matter

Yod י

He ה

Vav ו

He ה

This name, known as the Tetragrammaton (meaning "four letters"), has been a focal point in understanding the Creator's identity. These letters are **Yod, He, Vav, He (see above)**.

The Paleo-Hebrew Version of the Name:

𐤆 Yod

𐤄 He

𐤅 Vav

𐤄 He

This breakdown can be interpreted as "**Behold the Hand, Behold the Nail**," suggesting a deep connection between these symbols and the Creator's name. The repetition of "behold" might also imply a continuous or renewed revelation, reflecting the Creator's ongoing presence and involvement in the world.

Yah-an Acceptable Name

"**Yah**" is a shortened form of the Tetragrammaton and is often used in ancient texts and scriptural references. It appears in names like "**Yah**udah" (**Judah**) and in phrases such as "Hallelu**jah**" (**Hallelu Yah**—remember there was no 'J'), which means "**Praise Yah**."

"**Yah**" in scripture:

Psalms 106:48, The Scriptures

"Blessed be Yahuah Elohim of Yisra'ĕl from everlasting to everlasting! And all the people shall say, 'Amĕn!' Praise <u>Yah</u>!"

Again in,

Psalms 68:4

"Sing to Elohim, sing praises to His Name. Raise up a highway for Him Who rides through the deserts, By His Name <u>Yah</u>, And exult before Him."

In recognizing these names, it's evident that each carries profound meaning, inviting us into a deeper understanding of our Creator's character and His relationship with humanity. While the term "God" has been widely used in translation, let's embrace the **sacredness of Yahuah's name with reverence and** awe, acknowledging Yah's uniqueness and majesty. Let our speech reflect the honor due to Him who reigns supreme over all creation.

The Name: A Connection to the Symbols

The Creator's name, "**Yahuah**," which means "**Behold the Hand, Behold the Nail**," hints at the Savior's role. The "**Nail**" symbolizes the **Savior's sacrifice**, linking the Creator's name to the Son's mission of redemption. In the next section, we'll explore how the Son's name reflects this profound connection.

Yahushua

יהושע

Yah-hoo-shoo-ah

OYW94Z

The Son

The Messiah

I believe the following verse is Yah telling us exactly what the Messiah's name is.

In Zechariah 6:9-13, we read:

"**And the word of Yahuah came unto me, saying, 'Take of them of the captivity, even of Heldai, of Tobijah, and of Jedaiah, which are come from Babylon, and come thou the same day, and go into the house of Josiah the son of Zephaniah; Then take silver and gold, and <u>make crowns</u>, and <u>set them upon the head of Yehoshua (Joshua)</u> the son of Josedech, the high priest;' And speak unto him <u>saying</u>, 'Thus** speaketh the Elohim of hosts, saying, 'Behold the man whose name is The Branch; and he shall grow up out of his place, and he shall build the temple of Yahuah: Even he shall build the temple of the Lord; and he shall bear the glory, and shall sit and rule upon his throne; and he shall be a priest upon his throne: and the counsel of peace shall be between them both.'"

Joshua יהושע

Joshua (Yehoshua) means "Yahuah is salvation" or "Yahuah saves." Zechariah was specifically instructed to crown Joshua (Yehoshua) and proclaim, "Behold the man (Joshua) whose NAME is the BRANCH." This connection between the name Yahushua and the prophecy of The Branch suggests that the name of our Messiah is intricately woven into scripture.

Jeremiah 23:5 echoes this connection:

"Behold, the days are coming," says Yahuah, "That I will raise to David a Branch of righteousness; A King shall reign and prosper, And execute judgment and righteousness in the earth."

When we examine the prophecy in Zechariah 6:12 and compare it to Jeremiah 23:5, we find that the same Hebrew word, **"Branch"** is used in both passages. This word is a title often associated with the **Messiah**, making the connection between the two verses significant. In Zechariah, the crowning of Joshua (**Yehoshua**) and the proclamation, "Behold the man whose name is The Branch," hints at a deeper meaning. It suggests that the name of the future Messiah, who is referred to as, "The Branch," will be the same as Yehoshua. This reinforces the idea that Zechariah 6 is a clear Messianic prophecy, indicating that the Messiah will bear the name Yehoshua.

Yahushua – A Detailed Breakdown

Tetragrammaton and the Name "Yahushua"

The Tetragrammaton (**YHWH or YHVH**) is embedded within the name "**Yahushua**," as the "**Yahu**" portion directly refers to the name of the **Creator**. This connection emphasizes that the name "**Yahushua**" carries the divine name within it, linking the person bearing this name to the Creator directly.

This construction is not just a name but a declaration of identity and purpose, indicating that **the one named Yahushua is directly tied to the mission of bringing salvation from Yahuah.**

Yahushua יהושע

The name "**Yahushua**" in Hebrew is composed of two primary elements:

- "**Yahu**": The sacred name of the Creator.

- "**Shua**": This means "salvation" or "to save."

Together, "**Yahushua**" translates to "**Yahuah is salvation**" or "Yahuah saves."

In the Paleo-Hebrew representation of "**Yahushua**," the "**shua**" sound is made up of specific letters that correspond to the ancient script.

Joshua and The Messiah in Hebrew

Joshua (Yehoshua) in Hebrew: יהושע

Messiah (Yahushua) in Hebrew: יהושע

When I saw this I was convinced I was on the right track.

Yahushua Breakdown-In Paleo-Hebrew

Yod ㄥ

Hey �

Vav Y

Shin ㄩ

Ayin O

OYWY�3ㄥ

Yod: Represents a hand or arm, symbolizing action or creation.

Hey: Represents "**behold**" or revelation, and also conveys the breath or spirit of life.

Vav: Represents a **nail** or hook, symbolizing connection or securing.

Shin: This letter is often associated with the idea of "teeth," which can symbolize something sharp or powerful. It can represent **consuming, destruction, or**

pressing. In a spiritual sense, it might symbolize the power and authority of the Savior to overcome and destroy sin.

Ayin: This letter symbolizes an "**eye**" or "to see," possibly representing the Savior's **watchfulness, insight, or understanding** and producing the "a" sound in "**shua**."

These Paleo-Hebrew characters combine to form the name "Yahushua," with the "shua" part represented by the letters **Shin** and **Ayin**, creating the "**shua**" sound.

"O" vs. "U" Sound

YahOah/YahOshua: Reflects the influence of Masoretic vowel points, leading to an "O" sound in these names. The correct spelling is, **Yahuah/Yahushua**, which represents names based on ancient pronunciation, using the "U" sound as in names like "Yahudah" (Judah).

The most beautiful revelation I received from today's Sabbath study is this...

In The Scriptures Bible,

Exodus 23:20-21

"See, I am sending a Messenger before you to guard you in the way and to bring you into the place which I have prepared. Be on guard before Him and obey His voice. Do not rebel against Him, for He is not going to pardon your transgression, for <u>My Name is in Him</u>."

YAHUshua means YAHUah Saves!

It's perfect, Yahu+ ~~Yeho~~shua=Yahushua

Let us close in prayer...

Yahuah, Our Mighty Creator,

What a wonderful Sabbath we've had! As we rested our bodies, we also opened our hearts to learn more about You. We are deeply grateful for everything You provide and for the sacred time, You have set aside each week for us to commune with You and with each other. This blessing is truly understood by those who observe the Sabbath faithfully. Our love for You knows no bounds, and we worship You with every fiber of our being.

As we embark on the week ahead, may our actions be pleasing to You. Grant us the wisdom to seize every opportunity to serve You and to sow seeds of spiritual growth that You may nurture. We humbly ask for Your protection over us and our families, keeping us safe from harm.

In Yahushua's name. Amen!

Ninth Sabbath Day

Almighty Yah,

We seek Your blessings on this sacred Sabbath day. Guide us into Your presence and prepare our hearts with Your truth. We honor and cherish this day, set apart for rest and reflection in Your divine presence. As we gather to worship You, continue to reveal Your wisdom and guidance, empowering us to follow You with unwavering devotion. May our actions and attitudes provoke curiosity in those around us, drawing them closer to Your commandments and the path of righteousness. Your Word is love and truth, lighting our way in this world. Help us to worship You in every aspect of our lives, glorifying Your name through our words and deeds.

In the name of Yahushua, we pray. Amen.

A Transformative Friday Night

Journal Entry: As the sun sets on this Friday evening, my entire inner self calms down. The outside lights, perfectly timed, switch on as the sun disappears. I know the deer are entering the property, eager to munch on every flower I painstakingly planted over the past week. My doorbell camera captures countless videos of them leisurely hanging out on the porch, taking their time to eat as if they owned the place.

Growing up in the city, deer were never something I had to consider. I never even saw one unless I was at a zoo. My world was filled with pavement, a single tree, a few flower pots on the porch, and the ever-present glow of streetlights. In New England, many nights the windows were left open while I slept; the sounds of sirens, people, and vehicles soothed me to sleep. Later on, living further north, in New Hampshire, the quiet was unsettling at first, the darkness even more so. But over time, whether in the city, beach, or country, I've learned to appreciate the peace I have found in Him. Where else can you find such peace on this earth? I said, "nowhere," until I observed Shabbat. I didn't truly understand the beautiful balance and peace in my life — it is a true blessing.

When Shabbat begins, an instant peace washes over me. For the next 24 hours, I can rest and focus on Him. It's perfect. I am profoundly grateful for Yahuah's unwavering patience with me. I wonder what took me so long to see the truth? It must have been a mix of pride and pure laziness, leaving my salvation up to pastors and preachers as if they held the power.

From my earliest memories, the Word has been a constant in my life, dating back to when I was about five. My Mémère faithfully took me to church, where I absorbed the rituals and teachings of Catholicism. Serving as an altar girl alongside my uncle, the school's priest, was a weekly highlight. Those early years in Catholic school, with plaid jumpers, knee-high socks, and innocent joys, laid the foundation for my faith.

But adolescence brought change. The innocence of childhood birthday parties and playground games gave way to the complexities of teenage hormones and the separation from childhood friends. High school marked a new chapter filled with uncertainty and a growing sense of independence. The daily routine of school, bus rides, and monotony became my norm, yet I felt an underlying shift. Freshman year passed quickly, but summer brought significant change. It was this summer I decided I wouldn't be going back to Catholic school.

By the end of freshman year, everything started to feel unfamiliar. The structured routine that defined my life for 13 years was gone. The familiar faces, the comfort of the same building, and the security of a known faith had vanished. It felt like being thrust into the world without a safety net. The teenage years can feel like wandering through the devil's playground—full of confusion, isolation, and a sense of invincibility, creating the perfect breeding ground for bad choices that can affect your entire life. It's a time of separation from all you knew, a time when doubt and rebellion can easily lead one astray from all that kept them safe and secure.

Yet, no matter what was happening in the world around me, I always found comfort in Him. Was I obedient? Umm, no! There were years that I ran to Him only when things went wrong. Then there were times during some of life's devastations when I submerged myself in the Word and in prayer. But looking back, so much was missing in my walk because in Catholic school you learn the 'to do,s' and not the importance of the relationship. Priests do all the studying for you; you just have to sit in a pew and pay attention for an hour.

Not a bad deal. If my life hadn't changed enough at this point, I was about to enter into a spiritual change that would shake all I thought I knew about God and Jesus.

During a call to a friend, a party line interrupted — a phenomenon those from the '80s will understand. Amidst the ringing, I heard a voice on the other end, and we struck up a conversation. We exchanged numbers, and he invited my friend's group to a Bible study his dad was hosting at their house. A Bible study? At someone's house? I remember thinking how odd it seemed.

That unexpected invitation was the beginning of a journey that would eventually lead me to the truth, the peace of Shabbat, and a deeper relationship with Yahuah.

It was then I learned there were 'other' denominations other than Catholic. I saw the bible for the first time and wouldn't you know that the first bible study was about the book of Revelation. Well, if that didn't scare the Catholic out of me, nothing would. I was so shocked, I had never heard of this book-Revelation. It talks about the end, what end? Why and when does this end happen? I was 100% filled with curiosity driven by fear, but that was okay because it was a path I needed to be on. Sadly, I stayed in Babylon for 40 years under the comfort and security of "once saved always saved, saved under grace, we are not under the law, we cannot work for our salvation" doctrines. As I am typing this, I just realized I was under this falseness for 40 years. 15 years old to 55 years old. My first Sabbath day was September 9th, 2023 at 55 years old. Wow! If I can parallely put my life along with the Israelites... I left Catholicism, they left Egypt, I was in a false church for 40 years, they were in the desert for 40 years... 40 years of complete stubbornness!

That week in September, Yahuah woke me up thinking about the 10 commandments and I pondered why didn't I ever think of them. Walking over to that plaque in my kitchen, which sat on the walk inches from my coffee pot, a place I visited faithfully every morning of my life and never bothered to even look at the decoration that, I myself, nailed to the wall. Until that morning and when I ever came across the 4th commandment ... Well here I am. Now I have finally arrived in Truth! HalleluYah!!! Like way back when in my teenage years, when I was called to change. I believe the difference between then and now is the reverence for the 10 commandments. Like the Israelites, I thought I could just wander about acting like I make the rules. Now, I clearly see the depth and blessings of following the commandments.

Without them we are lost, so lost. Our Messiah came to show us how to **abide** in Him by keeping them. Through Yahushua, we can follow His example and His was perfect. He loved perfectly, without blemish, and followed laws, statutes, and commandments. Yah's **grace** was sufficient, to give us **all** a chance to enter into His kingdom by His Son. **He is the Way, the Truth, and the Life!**

Brothers and sisters, Yahushua's life points to the commandments. **Grace** does not mean we don't have to keep the commandments and abiding in him is a continuous, ongoing thing.

The Commandments - Not Abolished

John 15:10-15

"If you keep my commandments, you will abide in my love, just as I have kept my Father's commandments and abide in his love. These things I have spoken to you, that my joy may be in you, and that your joy may be full."

'Abide' in The Strong's Concordance: verb; equivalent to not to depart, not to leave, to continue to be present, to maintain unbroken fellowship.

It is absolutely clear you must stay in Him, continuously adhering to the commandments and when you find that you've sinned, confess and repent quickly, asking for forgiveness in Yahushua's name. Once you become aware of that sin, "go and sin no more." Do not keep returning to that sin, let Him change you.

Are you questioning "once saved, always saved" at this point? I was after I read, "We must abide" and that made it clear. What if you stopped 'abiding?' Which would mean you stop keeping the commandments. Pay attention to these beautiful instructions given to you from the One that loves you the MOST, your Creator!

Below are the 10 simple requests from our Father. I ask that you put away all your doctrinal minds and search for the truth with me. This is a huge topic of discussion within the communities I have encountered on my short, yet powerful, revealing journey of 9 weeks.

1. Worship only one God.

2. Do not make or worship idols.

3. Do not misuse the name of God.

4. Remember the Sabbath day and keep it holy.

5. Honor your parents.

6. Do not murder.

7. Do not commit adultery.

8. Do not steal.

9. Do not bear false witness against your neighbor.

10. Do not covet your neighbor's possessions.

I don't even know where to start on this topic because I hear so many wrong opinions used to refute the fact that the commandments are for today.

The best way to continue in this chapter is to list all the reasons I hear to NOT keep the commandments. **Let's take a look at the most common comebacks most of us hear and examine them.** If we take the opportunity to study these, what I call, comebacks, then we will know how to answer someone when they question us. Not to be right, but to plant seeds and turn their eyes to the Truth, the Instructions, and the Way!

The commandments are not for today. I think this one is the most dangerous. It cancels out any accountability to the way we should be living as **set-apart** children. Without it, you can be self-serving, deciding what Yah wants for us, which is another way of YOU making the rules. For humble servants of the Most High, we should want to follow the commandments, for they are "not grievous" as the bible states. The denial of them creates no room for discussion. How can we discuss them and move towards agreement if the conversation ends before it begins? All you have to do is read the 'red letters' (Yahushua's words) alone and you can see Yahushua's plea to follow them. In John 14:15 He says, "If you love me, keep my commandments." If there is another definition for "keep" that I am unaware of please let me know.

We are not under the law anymore. The Biblical Concept of Lawlessness In Hebrew refers to **lawlessness** and conveys **rebellion** against Yahuah's order and commandments. It appears in the Old Testament to describe acts of rebellion and **disobedience** that lead to **chaos** and **disorder**. As believers, we are called to embrace the commandments and reject lawlessness. Lawlessness = the absence of commandments.

Jesus fulfilled the law. He came to reunite, renew, and fulfill the scriptures, not to do away with anything that **Yahuah has established for all generations.**

Which means forever, from beginning to end. ALL GENERATIONS means just that. Yahushua states He did not do away with the Law of our Creator. Obviously, there's a misunderstanding of the word "fulfill" here.

Misinterpretation of Matthew 5:17-18:

"Yahushua said, 'Do not think that I have come to abolish the Law or the Prophets; I have not come to abolish them but to fulfill them.'"

Some interpret "fulfill" to mean that Yahushua's coming nullifies the commandments. However, "fulfill" means that our Messiah completed His purpose and provided a perfect example of obedience. He came to fulfill the Word, and the prophecies and made the plan complete, hence... "do not think I have come to abolish the law or the prophets."

In this context, "the law" refers to the Torah (the commandments and instructions given to the Israelites), and "the Prophets" refers to the prophetic writings in the Old Testament. Yahushua emphasized the importance of upholding Yah's moral and ethical standards while also pointing to Himself as the ultimate fulfillment of Yah's plan.

From a Torah observant perspective, this means that while certain ceremonial and ritual aspects of the law (such as sacrifices and temple practices) are no longer necessary because of Yahushua's sacrifice, the moral and ethical principles remain relevant. Yahushua IS the perfect embodiment of Yahuah's righteousness.

There's no way we can keep all the rules, all 613 of them. There is some debate as to who first came up with 613 as the number of commandments/laws. The 613 rules are a significant part of Jewish religious and cultural practices. These rules are derived from the Torah and cover a wide range of topics. They consist of 248 'things to do' and 365 'things to avoid.' While there is no specific verse in the Bible that lists all 613 rules, they serve as a guide for righteous living. Not all are for men and not all are for women, some rules are for farmers only, so in no way are they ALL to be kept.

Commandments are for today, except the 4th one. This has to be my all-time fav! It makes no sense to me, none. So you finally find those who believe the commandments are for today and then claim the 4th one is not for today? Does this make sense? The picking and choosing needs to go already! I have touched on this one several times throughout this book. We have talked about how "resting in Him" does not mean we do not keep the Sabbath. We learned that the Sabbath day was from creation to the end of time — when we are on the new earth. You cannot cherry-pick commandments to self-serve yourself or your agendas.

I believe in the Sabbath day, but it can be any day you want it to be. But can it? Again, who is deciding, you or your Father? So, if you take Wednesday off this week, you have to take every Wednesday off to keep your 7th day Sabbath? For the rest of your life? Again, this is not how Yah wants. REMEMBER to KEEP the 7TH DAY holy.

How do we know Saturday is the 7th day? Currently, I believe it is Saturday this year (2024.) As discussed in the previous chapter, the calendar we know today is not the real way to tell time. I am currently studying this and feel I can't give a correct answer right now. What I do know, today, the majority of the world uses what is known as the Gregorian calendar, named after Pope Gregory Xlll, who introduced it in 1582. Knowing its source I think we are safe to say it's probably incorrect.

The Sabbath isn't sunset to sunset, it's dawn to dawn or sunrise to sunset. As discussed in the previous chapter, I keep sunset Friday to sunset Saturday (this is something I am still researching as well).

We are under grace now. The fact that we even have the opportunity to enter Yah's kingdom is His grace! We find His grace all through the scripture of Him trying to reconcile His people back to Him, ultimately knowing that we would need a Messiah. A Messiah to show us how to live, how Yah expects and desires us to live a holy, set-apart life.

Only for Israel. Salvation is for everyone. Yahushua came for the Jews and the Gentiles. We are grafted into Israel making us all Yah's children. Better yet, the commandments were made way before Jews, Gentiles, and Israelites existed. Do you think all Jews are saved just because they call themselves Jews? No! They, too, have to be saved to enter into the kingdom and become Israel. Israel is a people, not a land.

If we keep the commandments, we are working for our salvation. How are you set apart? Are you acting any different than a gentile (non-saved) if you're walking around doing nothing different? Are you abiding in Him? Abiding ... a continuation of work, a verb, an action to stay connected to the Vine, and if you don't, you can become the branch that is cast away.

John 15:6

"If a man abide not in me, he is cast forth as a branch, and is withered; and men gather them, and cast them into the fire, and they are burned."

John 15:9-12

"As the Father has loved me, so have I loved you. Abide in my love. If you keep my commandments, you will abide in my love, just as I have kept my Father's commandments and abide in his love. These things I have spoken to you, that my joy may be in you, and that your joy may be full. "This is my commandment, that you love one another as I have loved you."

James 2:14-26 Faith and Deeds

"'What good is it, my brothers and sisters, if someone claims to have faith but has no deeds? Can such faith save them? Suppose a brother or a sister is without clothes and daily food. If one of you says to them, 'Go in peace; keep warm and well fed,' but does nothing about their physical needs, what good is it? In the same way, <u>faith by itself, if it is not accompanied by action, is dead.</u>But someone will say, "You have faith; I have deeds.""

"Show me your faith without deeds, and I will show you my faith by my deeds. You believe that there is one God. Good! Even the demons believe that—and shudder."

"You foolish person, do you want evidence that faith without deeds is useless? Was not our father Abraham considered righteous for what he did when he offered his son Isaac on the altar? You see that his faith and his actions were working together, and his faith was made complete by what he did. And the scripture was fulfilled that says, "Abraham believed God, and it was credited to him as righteousness," and he was called God's friend. <u>You see that a person is considered righteous by what they do and not by faith alone."</u>

" In the same way, was not even Rahab the prostitute considered <u>righteous for what she did</u> when she gave lodging to the spies and sent them off in a different direction? As the body without the spirit is dead, so faith without deeds is dead."

Revelation 22:12-14

"And behold, I come shortly, and my reward is with me, <u>to give to every man according as his work shall be.</u> I am Alpha and Omega, the beginning and the end, the first and the last. Blessed *are* they, that do his Commandments, that their right may be in the tree of Life, and may enter in through the gates into the City."

We only have to keep two commandments. This comeback baffles me. We need to read the entire book, to get context and understanding.

Matthew 22:36-40

"Master, which is the great Commandment in the law? Jesus said unto him, 'You shall love the Lord your God with all your heart, and with all your soul, and with all your mind. This is the first and great commandment. And the second is like unto it, You shall love your neighbour as yourself.' On these two commandments hang ALL the law and the prophets."

Love God + Love Your Neighbor as Yourself = The 10 Commandments.

Looking at the 10 Commandments as a whole, it is generally understood and agreed that the 1st through 4th Commandments have to do with our relationship with Yah, and the 5th through 10th Commandments have to do with our relationships with other people. Yahushua affirmed this in Matthew 22:40 when He said, *"All the Law and the Prophets hang on these two commandments"* (referring to the commands to love Yahuah and love your neighbor).

So what does this all prove? ALL the law which **includes the Sabbath,** hung on these two Commandments in the Old Testament which no one can dispute, and while Yahushua quotes from the Old Testament, He still says ALL the law hung on these two greatest Commandments. So what has changed? Absolutely nothing! Everything Yah wrote in stone remains totally unchanged just as Yahushua promised in 20. This verse scares me for those who are telling people to forget about just ONE commandment.

Matthew 5:17-20

"Do not think that I came to destroy the Law or the Prophets. I did not come to destroy but to fulfill. For assuredly, I say to you, till heaven and earth pass away, one jot or one tittle will by no means pass from the law till all is fulfilled. Whoever therefore breaks one of the least of these commandments, and teaches men so, shall be called least in the kingdom of heaven; but whoever does and teaches them, he shall be called great in the kingdom of heaven. For I say to you, that unless your righteousness exceeds

the righteousness of the scribes and Pharisees, you will by no means enter the kingdom of heaven."

Let me ask you, friends... on judgment day what are you being judged against? What guidelines will Yah, who is a just Father, use? How do you know when you are sinning if you don't have the commandments to use to search your own hearts, minds, and actions? The Bible speaks of warnings against 'lawless' people and people that practice 'lawlessness.' Let's look up what 'lawlessness' means.

Looking in The Strong's Concordance for the Greek meaning of lawlessness I found this: lawlessness, iniquity, disobedience, sin.

Disobedient to what- yourself? Sin-what is sin? How do you know what sin is? If it weren't for the commandments you wouldn't have a reference to what sin is.

Are you all getting exhausted with these common comebacks when you try to explain why you honor the Sabbath? It is exhausting but remember we were there before. They don't know, but the fact they ask us is what we prayed for. Let our actions bring about curiosity in hopes we can plant a seed. Don't get weary, it is our pleasure to have Yah within us noticed.

"Why were my eyes, your eyes opened and not others?" I ask myself all the time. I recently read a verse that shook me a bit because I don't understand why Yah would do this, but who am I to question His ways?

2 Thessalonians 2:9-16 ISR TS2009

"The coming of the lawless one is according to the working of Satan, with all power and signs and wonders of falsehood, and with all deceit of unrighteousness in those perishing, because they did not receive the love of the truth, in order for them to be saved. And for this reason <u>Elohim sends them a working of delusion</u>, for them to believe the falsehood, in order that all should be judged who did not believe the truth, but have delighted in the unrighteousness.

But we ought to give thanks to Elohim always for you, brothers, beloved by the Master, because Elohim from the beginning chose you for deliverance through set-apartness of Spirit and belief in the truth, to which He called you by our Good News, for the obtaining of the esteem of our Master Messiah. So, then, brothers, stand fast and hold the traditions which you were taught, whether by word or by our letter.

And our Master Messiah Himself, and our Elohim and Father, who has loved us and given us everlasting encouragement and good expectation through favour, encourage your hearts and establish you in every good word and work."

My eyes watered when I typed out that verse. I am so full of gratitude to be set apart. I'm so grateful for you, that you are here with me on this journey.

Now to close with a word of prayer:

Heavenly Father,

We are so filled with gratitude that You chose us. You are worthy to be praised for all the days of our existence. Let us be a reflection of righteousness and not a stumbling block for those around us. Help us speak Your truth, not our own.

Give us the words to use, the eyes to see, and the ears to hear so we can glorify You more and more. Strengthen our faith and guide our steps, so we may walk in Your ways and be a light to others.

Protect us and our families as we go into the world, and not be of the world. Grant us wisdom and courage to face challenges with grace and to uphold Your commandments in all we do.

Fill our hearts with love and compassion, so we may serve others selflessly and bring honor to Your name. May Your presence be with us always, guiding and sustaining us.

Amen, amen. In Yahushua's name.

Tenth Sabbath Day

Let's enter into the Sabbath with a prayer:

Father, Yahuah Elohim, we give You thanks and praise for all You have revealed to us over the past ten weeks. Please guide us as we transform into Your truth and break free from the chains of false doctrine that have held us for so long. Let us rejoice in finding the Truth, which has led us to the Way and into Life—a life with You everlasting. Help us to plant seeds that will build communities so we can fellowship as You have always intended. All glory, honor, and praise to You, Father Yah.

In Yahushua's mighty name.

Journal Entry: This is my last entry, marking the beginning of my new way of life. I have loved this journey and cannot imagine anyone wanting to leave it once they've experienced it. At the start of this journey, I was filled with so much peace because I found a relationship with my Father that I'd never had before. However, I was also angry—angry at the lies and deceit the enemy has deeply rooted in our lives, whether through pastors, parents, or our laziness in not going directly to the Word. It was a stronghold, for sure.

I am now committed and delighted to walk into the second part of my life in truth, acknowledging the commands He set for us to live a holier life, with discipline and respect for His instructions. These always lead to a simpler, more peaceful, and more joyous life. It was overwhelming at first, relearning things I thought I knew and facing the unknown. Can I say my foundation became both solid and shaken at the same time? I feel more grounded now that I'm in the truth, but I also feel overwhelmed realizing how much I still have to learn.

As I approach the 10th week, it was recommended that I look into the Feast Days, and honestly, I'm not certain about them yet, but I am drawn to them. They are so fascinating and meaningful that I think we should all pay attention to them. I'm not sure how to word this, but if you go through the Feasts, you see a glimpse of the past and a glimpse of the future. It's like the entire story of the Bible is being played out in these seven Feasts... OH MY... 7!! Just like the days of creation, and maybe like the beginning to the end—like Genesis to Revelation.

Starting with the first Feast, having to select the perfect Lamb...??? Yahushua—the perfect Lamb! Placed on the doorposts... like Yahushua "stands at the door and knocks?" Oh, and "door" is represented by the number 4 in Hebrew and guys... get this... the 4th commandment is the Sabbath. Is the Sabbath the door to the Way? Oh my, and He is the WAY!!! Let's head into the study of the Feasts... This is making me tear up... When scripture paints a picture in your mind and your heart like this, it can be so emotional. Thank you, Yahuah! Thank you!

The Seven Feasts

1. Passover (Pesach)

Scripture Reference: Exodus 12:1-14; Leviticus 23:4-8

Timing: 14th day of the first month (Nisan).

Rules: A lamb without blemish was to be selected and sacrificed.

The blood of the lamb was to be placed on the doorposts and lintel of each house.

The lamb was to be roasted and eaten with unleavened bread and bitter herbs.

No leaven (yeast) was to be found in the house for seven days.

Foreshadow: The sacrificial lamb represents Yahushua, whose blood saves us from spiritual death.

Fulfillment: Yahushua's crucifixion as the Passover Lamb.

Prophecy: Isaiah 53:7 - "He was oppressed, and he was afflicted, yet he opened not his mouth; he is brought as a lamb to the slaughter..." This prophecy describes the suffering Messiah, fulfilled by Yahushua's death.

2. Feast of Unleavened Bread (Chag HaMatzot)

Scripture Reference: Leviticus 23:6-8

Timing: 15th to 21st day of Nisan.

Rules: The feast lasts for seven days, starting on the 15th of Nisan.

No leavened bread is to be eaten during this period.

The first and seventh days are to be observed as holy convocations with no customary work.

Foreshadow: The removal of leaven symbolizes sinlessness.

Fulfillment: Yahushua's sinless body was in the tomb during this feast.

Prophecy: Psalm 16:10 - "For You will not leave my soul in Sheol, nor will You allow Your Holy One to see corruption." This messianic prophecy is fulfilled as Yahushua's body did not decay.

3. Feast of Firstfruits

Scripture Reference: Leviticus 23:9-14

Timing: The day after the Sabbath following Passover.

Rules: The first sheaf of the barley harvest is to be offered to Yahuah.

The offering must include a lamb without blemish, flour mixed with oil, and wine.

Foreshadow: Symbolizes Yahushua's resurrection, marking the beginning of the spiritual harvest.

Fulfillment: Yahushua's resurrection as the first fruits of those who have fallen asleep.

Prophecy: Psalm 22:22 - "I will declare Your name to My brethren; amid the assembly I will praise You." This verse, referring to the resurrection, points to Yahushua's victory over death.

4. Feast of Weeks (Shavuot or Pentecost)

Scripture Reference: Leviticus 23:15-21

Timing: 50 days after the Feast of First Fruits.

Rules: Two loaves of bread made with leaven are to be offered, along with animal sacrifices.

A holy convocation is to be observed with no customary work.

Foreshadow: Represents the coming of the Holy Spirit and the birth of the Church.

Fulfillment: The descent of the Holy Spirit during Pentecost.

Prophecy: Joel 2:28-29 - "And it shall come to pass afterward that I will pour out My Spirit on all flesh..." This prophecy is directly quoted by Peter in Acts 2:17, fulfilled by the outpouring of the Holy Spirit at Pentecost.

5. Feast of Trumpets (Yom Teruah or Rosh Hashanah)

Scripture Reference: Leviticus 23:23-25

Timing: 1st day of the seventh month (Tishrei).

Rules: The day is to be marked by the blowing of trumpets.

A holy convocation is to be observed with no customary work.

Foreshadow: The blowing of trumpets signals Yahushua's return.

Fulfillment: Points to the future return of Yahushua.

Prophecy: 1 Corinthians 15:52 - "In a moment, in the twinkling of an eye, at the last trumpet. For the trumpet will sound, and the dead will be raised incorruptible..." This prophecy describes the future resurrection and transformation of believers at Yahushua's second coming.

6. Day of Atonement (Yom Kippur)

<u>Scripture Reference</u>: Leviticus 23:26-32

<u>Timing</u>: 10th day of the seventh month (Tishrei).

<u>Rules</u>: The day is to be marked by fasting, repentance, and the high priest making atonement for the people.

A holy convocation is to be observed with no customary work.

<u>Foreshadow</u>: Represents final judgment and atonement.

<u>Fulfillment</u>: Yahushua's sacrifice provides ultimate atonement.

<u>Prophecy</u>: Zechariah 12:10 - "And I will pour on the house of David and on the inhabitants of Jerusalem the spirit of grace and supplication; then they will look on Me whom they pierced..." This prophecy is often connected to the Day of Atonement and points to Israel's future recognition of Yahushua as the Messiah.

7. Feast of Tabernacles (Sukkot)

Scripture Reference: Leviticus 23:33-43

Timing: 15th to 21st day of the seventh month (Tishrei).

Rules: The feast lasts for seven days, starting on the 15th of Tishrei.

Temporary shelters (sukkahs) are to be built and lived in during the feast.

The first and eighth days are to be observed as holy convocations with no customary work.

Foreshadow: Symbolizes Yahuah's presence dwelling among His people.

Fulfillment: Yahushua's future reign during the Messianic Kingdom.

Prophecy: Zechariah 14:16 - "And it shall come to pass that everyone who is left of all the nations which came against Jerusalem shall go up from year to year to worship the King, Yahuah of hosts, and to keep the Feast of Tabernacles." This prophecy points to a future time when all nations will celebrate Sukkot in the Messianic Kingdom.

Honoring the biblical festivals today serves a profound purpose in the spiritual lives of believers. These feasts are more than historical observances; they are living reminders of Yahuah's mighty acts of salvation and provision. Each festival, from Passover to the Feast of Tabernacles, commemorates significant moments in the biblical narrative, such as the Israelites' deliverance from Egypt, while also pointing to Yahushua's redemptive work. For example, Passover not only recalls the original exodus but also foreshadows Yahushua as the Lamb of Yahuah, whose sacrifice delivers us from the bondage of sin. Observing these festivals helps believers align with Yahuah's timeline, deepening their understanding of His prophetic fulfillment in Yahushua.

Additionally, these feasts provide structured opportunities for spiritual renewal, reflection, and community building. They serve as set times for repentance, thanksgiving, and celebration, fostering a sense of unity and shared identity among believers. By honoring these appointed times, believers connect with the rich heritage of faith passed down through generations, participate in Yahuah's ongoing redemptive plan, and anticipate the future fulfillment of His promises, such as Yahushua's return and the establishment of His Kingdom.

I hear different opinions on this topic—some say we should observe the feasts, while others say we don't have to. I have to admit, whenever I hear "we don't have to do it," I become a bit suspicious. I've heard that all my life and I know too well that "we don't have to do it" could be misleading. So, I dig deeper. I investigate, research, and study to show myself approved, seeking His truth.

After gaining all this knowledge alongside you, I'm humbled and blown away by how perfectly orchestrated these feasts are. I can't help but feel that there are important messages within them that we need to understand. This realization has also led me to question our current celebrations—specifically, the pagan holidays that have become our Christian holidays. Why do we celebrate them?

Pagan Rituals Unaware

It dawned on me last Easter that people were also celebrating Passover. I never noticed something like this before until now. What confused me the most was that people were observing Passover on different days. How do they now know the day to celebrate it? I couldn't honor any celebration when I didn't understand it.   At that time I put off learning about the feast days until now because another is approaching, and I want to understand it. Recently I saw a teaching on different calendars so I think the confusion lies in the fact that they follow different calendars (which I'm also studying). Another confusing point was Christians celebrating Easter — a holiday focused on the crucifixion and resurrection—but they celebrated it well before the Passover celebration. Huh? Yahushua died at Passover, so you'd think Easter would coincide with Passover. It doesn't make sense, and I'm beginning to think I might not be celebrating these man-made, Rome-influenced holidays much longer. Let's dig a little deeper...

Pagan Holidays:

Easter has its roots in ancient pagan traditions, originally starting as a celebration of the Spring Equinox, a time when nature awakens from winter and the cycle of renewal begins. Anglo-Saxon pagans honored this period by invoking Ēostre or Ostara, the goddess of spring, dawn, and fertility. Fertility was crucial for the survival of communities, leading to festivals that likely included sex rituals and orgies. As Christianity spread, especially under Emperor Constantine I, these pagan rituals were gradually absorbed into Christian practices, merging the old traditions with new religious beliefs. Rabbits, or the bunny, are symbols of fertility and are linked to the pagan goddess Eostre, while eggs have long been universal symbols of fertility. The tradition of painting eggs, which dates back to ancient cultures like the Egyptians, Persians, and Romans, evolved into the widespread Easter egg decorating tradition seen today, blending ancient fertility symbols with modern customs.

Christmas celebrated on December 25th, is a holiday with roots in various pagan traditions incorporated into Christianity. Originally, this date aligned with the Roman festival of Saturnalia, a time of feasting, gift-giving, and revelry honoring the god Saturn. Additionally, the festival of Sol Invictus, celebrating the "Unconquered Sun," marked the winter solstice, symbolizing the return of longer days. Over time, these traditions blended with Christian practices, resulting in the modern celebration of Christmas.

Key elements of Christmas, such as decorating trees, exchanging gifts, and festive meals, have origins in these ancient pagan celebrations. The choice of December 25th was likely influenced by the desire to align Christian observances with existing winter festivals, creating a celebration that would resonate with both new converts and existing traditions.

Despite its pagan roots, Christmas today is widely recognized as a celebration of the birth of Jesus Christ.

There are many holidays and celebrations, such as Halloween, that we should carefully consider before partaking in. It's wise to examine any celebration not found in the Bible and determine for yourself and your family whether to honor these days. Remember that when you decorate your Christmas tree, paint Easter eggs, or carve pumpkins, you are engaging in practices rooted in ancient pagan rituals. What's most startling is that you don't even have to believe in Yahuah or the Messiah to celebrate these holidays; they are embraced by believers and atheists alike. How does this honor Yah? These traditions have become so entwined with worldly customs that they often leave no room for spiritual significance.

Celebrations to Revelations

Reflecting on my journey, I'm seeing the truth more clearly than ever. It's evident how deeply ingrained man-made traditions have been, leading me away from the ways of Yahuah Elohim. I've realized how much of what I've practiced is contrary to His intentions.

For years, I've engaged in holidays with pagan roots, participating in rituals far from the true celebrations

Yahuah has given us. These sacred feasts are filled with hidden treasures and profound knowledge, which we need to uncover.

This realization urges me to change, to seek and honor Yahuah's true ways, and to abandon the false practices that have obscured our understanding. Now, as I delve deeper, I wonder about the **dietary laws** and whether they've been done away with.

Clean and Unclean

The Bible instructs believers **not to eat unclean foods** for several key reasons. First, it is an act of obedience to Yahuah's commandments, showing a commitment to living according to His will.

These dietary laws also symbolize holiness and separation, distinguishing Yahuah's people from surrounding nations.

Leviticus 20:25-26

"You shall therefore distinguish between clean animals and unclean, between unclean birds and clean. And you shall not make yourselves abominable by beast or by bird, or by any kind of living thing that creeps on the ground, which I have separated from you as unclean. And you shall be holy

to Me, for I the Lord am holy, and have separated you from the peoples, that you should be Mine."

Additionally, some believe these laws promote physical health by avoiding animals that may carry diseases. Spiritually, avoiding unclean foods helps maintain purity, honoring the body as a temple of the Holy Spirit.

1 Corinthians 6:19-20

"Or do you not know that your body is the temple of the Holy Spirit who is in you, whom you have from God, and you are not your own?For you were bought at a price; therefore glorify God in your body and in your spirit, which are God's."

Finally, the distinction between clean and unclean animals serves as a symbolic lesson in discerning what is pure versus impure.

What are the Unclean Foods

The Bible, in Leviticus 11 and Deuteronomy 14, lists unclean foods as follows:

Unclean Land Animals: Those without split hooves or that do not chew cud, such as pigs, camels, rabbits, and hares.

Unclean Sea Creatures: Sea creatures lacking fins and scales, like shellfish (shrimp, crabs), catfish, and eels.

Unclean Birds: Certain birds like eagles, vultures, ravens, owls, and bats.

Unclean Insects: Most winged insects walking on all fours, except those with jointed legs for hopping (e.g., locusts, crickets).

Unclean Reptiles and Creatures: Creatures crawling on their belly or with many legs, such as snakes, lizards, and mice.

Reptiles and Insects

Reptiles and insects? I've got that one conquered. Oh, and thank you, Yah, for allowing ribeye steaks and chocolate cake!

These dietary laws were part of the covenant between Yahuah and the Israelites, distinguishing them from other nations and serving as a reminder of their holiness and separation from Yahuah. Yah wanted people to notice that we are different, not of the world, and act differently than the world. It's kind of cool to think of it that way. I know it arouses suspicion, curiosity, and sometimes transformation, leading one to the Creator.

Feasts, Foods, and Salvation Issues

Are keeping the feasts and eating clean salvation issues? That would depend on who you ask. I personally don't know yet, but I am always leaning toward doing what Yah wants me to do. Is it that hard? To me, whether or not it is a salvation issue I just want to be as pleasing as I can while in this fleshy body. I want to serve, to follow the footsteps of the Messiah, to do all I can to be set apart. This is definitely the way... the WAY... there it is again, lol, a meaning with meaning.

What a wonderful last Sabbath day to share with all of you. With every Sabbath day comes an opportunity to grow and learn something new. We have all been on a crash course, haven't we? Remember, the learning never ends, but there are those who will dig into the matter and those who will just hear it and walk away, whether it's true or not. How are they to know if they don't explore further? It's so important to know Him deeply, and what better way to grow your relationship with Him than by learning all you can about Him and striving to act like Him, to the best of your ability?

Let's close this Sabbath day with a prayer:

Yahuah Elohim,

We are so grateful for our time with you and our families. Thank you for Your patience with us as we start learning Your truth and the fact that it took so long for us to get here.

Please bless our endeavors as we walk forward down the narrow path towards You. Let us be surrounded by people who serve You and love You. Let us be leaders and teachers of the Word, planting seeds and sharing our testimonies of all You have done for us.

Protect us as we travel this road, even if it means walking alone, learning, praying, and embarking into new territories.

In Yahushua's wonderful, precious name. HalleluYah.

Our Paths Will Cross Again

As we say goodbye, I want to thank you all for being here. I know it was a lot of information to absorb, and like you, I had no idea one day a week would be so jam-packed with knowledge. The lies that were exposed, the rabbit holes we seldom came out of, and the amazement when all the truth came together—it's been a journey.

I believe the topics we went over are the classic first challenges that newbies face: the denial of the commandments and/or the Sabbath day, the names, the feasts, the pagan holidays, the churches, all the doctrinal falseness, calendars, days and times, the food, etc. I hope this memoir left you knowing you are not alone — we are facing a lot of the same things.

You have every right to question anything and everything I've said in this book. This is a new journey for me, a complete transformation — one that will likely transform many more times, and I'm sure of it. A teacher once told me, "Don't just believe me; go out and study it for yourself." I've followed that advice, and I trust you know this to be true as well.

Don't ever lose your love for Him! In everything we do, remember it's not supposed to be grievous; it's supposed to be fulfilling and something we want to do—just like we want to please anyone we are in a relationship with.

Don't let your new ways become legalistic; keep a sharp eye out for that. You cannot get caught up with your obedience becoming a checklist of rituals that must be achieved, but rather with an anticipation to partake. Yah loves us, and He is a Father of justice. He knows where our hearts are so stay humble, obedient, and open to learning. Stay honest with yourself because nothing is hidden from Him.

Don't let people tell you you're working for your salvation because we are not—salvation is working in us. On judgment day is when salvation comes, so "endure till the end," my brothers and sisters. Don't stop spreading the seeds of The Way and looking for a community to share Shabbat with.

Shalom, family!

John 3:35-36

The Father loves the Son and has given all things into his hand. Whoever believes in the Son has eternal life; whoever doesn't obey the Son shall not see life, but the wrath of Yahuah remains on him.

Walk like He walked